A GIFT FOR

FROM

ROCKING CHAIR TALES

Stories of Heart & Home

John William Smith

HOWARD
PUBLISHING CO.

Our purpose at Howard Publishing is to:
- *Increase faith* in the hearts of growing Christians
- *Inspire holiness* in the lives of believers
- *Instill hope* in the hearts of struggling people everywhere

Because He's coming again!

Rocking Chair Tales © 2005 by John William Smith
All rights reserved. Printed in the United States of America
Published by Howard Publishing Co., Inc.
3117 North 7th Street, West Monroe, Louisiana 71291-2227
www.howardpublishing.com

05 06 07 08 09 10 11 12 13 14   10 9 8 7 6 5 4 3 2 1

Compiled by Philis Boultinghouse
Cover and interior design by The DesignWorks Group, www.thedesignworksgroup.com

ISBN: 978-1-4767-7254-7

CONTENTS

There are only
two lasting bequests
we can hope
to give our children.
One of these is roots;
the other, wings.

H ODDING C ARTER III

INTRODUCTION

If you like good stories, I think you'll like this book. Stories of times gone by instill in us a consciousness of who we are—they give us a sense of *history,* and they help us understand the link that connects the past with the future.

When people see no relationship between themselves and their past, they feel isolated and disconnected. This feeling of disenfranchisement—which is sort of like a broken electrical circuit—destroys any sense of relationship by breaking down our bridges to the past and the future, leaving us isolated.

In order to reestablish our link with the past, we must retrace our steps. There is nothing to sustain us in our present direction—we must *go back.* We must rebuild basic family consciousness. I mean not only the immediate family of parents and children, but the extended family of grandparents, aunts, uncles, and cousins, and ultimately—

the human family.

In a society of fragmented families, far too many children grow to physical maturity with no sense of belonging, no investment in anything larger than themselves. *Storytelling* is a way of teaching and preserving family traditions, which allow children to see themselves as a part of and vital to an ongoing history. It gives them a definite connection to the past and obligates them to the future. Their whole concept of self-worth rests upon this identification.

Most of the stories in this book are from my childhood, and a few are from other people's experiences. People are always taking me off to the side and asking me if these stories really happened. Now, what kind of question is that? It sure takes the fun out of things. I think what is important is the *truth*.

For thousands of years, stories were the measure of truth, and they can still be used effectively in that way. Stories place truth in perspective. They give truth flavor by attaching names, faces, and geographical locations to abstract notions and emotional realities. I believe that all of these stories are true in that sense—

and in that sense, they are all parables.

I heard the following story from Fred Craddock, an instructor at the Candler School of Theology at Emory University in Atlanta, Georgia. It was originally told by Scott Momaday, a Kiowa Indian, writer, and literature professor at the University of Southern California.

Momaday says that when he was a small boy living in a Kiowa village, his father awakened him unexpectedly very early one morning. He told him to get up and get dressed. He led a very sleepy Momaday by the hand to the house of an old squaw. He left him there and promised to return that evening. This process was repeated over an extended period of time.

All day this ancient squaw told him the stories and sang him the songs of the Kiowa nation. She explained the rituals and the history of the Kiowa—how they began in a hollow log on the Yellowstone River, how they migrated westward. She told of wars with other tribes—of blizzards, cold, and famine. She told him of great chiefs, heroic deeds, and buffalo hunts. She told of the coming of the white man, the clash and the war, of moving north, of moving—always moving. She told of diminishing numbers, desperation, and finally, Fort Sill, Oklahoma. She told of the surrender, the reservation, confinement, despair—and the determination to survive.

Finally, the time of his education was over. Momaday said "I left her house a Kiowa. I knew what it meant to be a Kiowa. I knew who I was and who my people were, and I knew that I would always be a Kiowa."

Look back into your past; remember who you are and who your people were. And then tell those stories to your children. If you can't think of any, read the ones in this book; and in them you will find your own story. You can simply use them as a point of departure—

"That story reminds me of the time . . ."

It is my prayer that quite often, as you read this book, you will find yourself putting it down with a sigh and saying to yourself, "Yes, that is exactly the way it is." And it doesn't matter if the action was right or wrong—because if it was right, you need to imitate it; and if it was wrong, you need to avoid it.

My ultimate goal is that you look to the Giver and Creator of life—incorporating His wisdom and nature into your own—and become more and more like Him.

For where
your treasure is,
there your heart
will be also.

Luke 12:34

———

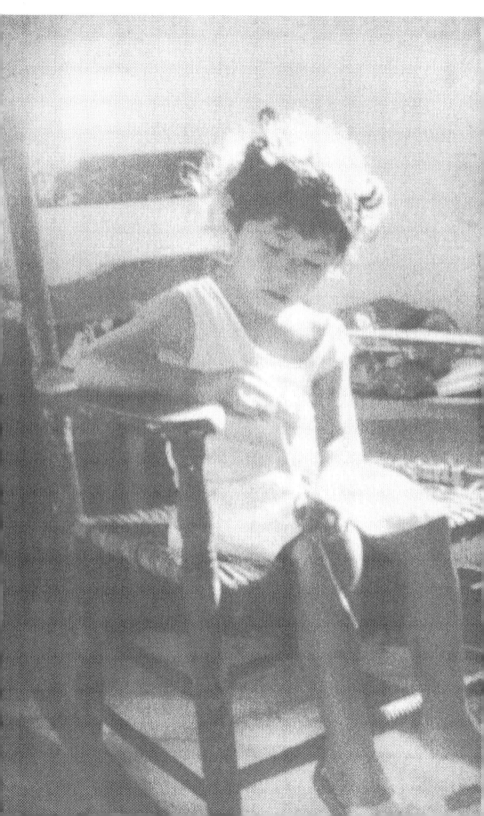

PART ONE

Parental Love

For the mother is
and must be,
whether she
knows it or not,
the greatest, strongest,
and most lasting teacher
her children have.

HANNAH WHITALL SMITH

Mother's Cherry Tree

My mother loved all growing things. We had apple trees, pear trees, a grape arbor, a rose arbor, tulips, lilacs, irises, and an annual garden. The Murdocks, who lived directly west of us, had a large cherry orchard. Although they gave us all the cherries we wanted, my mother was determined to have her own cherry tree. Accordingly, one fall we planted (I say "we," because I dug the hole)

a three-foot sapling. Mother fertilized, watered, watched over, pampered, and stroked that tree until it was a wonder it didn't die from too much attention. It was amazing how it grew, and in its second spring, it actually blossomed and bore cherries—not enough to make a pie, but my mother was so proud of the accomplishment that she nearly burst. She even carried some of those cherries in her purse to show her friends.

We always shopped at the A&P grocery store in Royal Oak. Fortunately for me, just down the street was Frantz & Sons Hardware. While my mother shopped, I wandered up and down the aisles of Frantz & Sons. It was a fascinating place. Great bins of nails, rows of hinges, racks of shovels, balls of twine—smells of feed, seed, leather goods—and a hundred other items all combined to make it a whole world in itself.

Inevitably, I was led to the fishing equipment, then the gun rack, and finally to the knife display case—which was a wooden cabinet with a glass door. I stood for long minutes gazing in wonder that there were so many fine things to be had. At the bottom of the knife case, there was one item in particular that attracted me. It was a belt hatchet—

just the right size for me.

It had a leather case that could be strapped right onto your belt for carrying purposes. I began to pester my mother about it. One day she actually went in to look at it, and I knew that my pleading was getting somewhere. It was a long process, but eventually she bought it for me.

I remember going around the yard whacking on things. It was exceedingly sharp. I whacked on old two-by-fours; I whacked apart an old crate that had been sitting behind the chicken coop—but it was all very dissatisfying. I wanted something more substantial to cut. All of the trees on our place were far too large for me to tackle with my hatchet—all except one: the cherry tree. As preposterous as this seems, the idea was probably enhanced by my schoolteacher telling us about George Washington cutting down the cherry tree. Since George was quite a hero, the idea of cutting down our cherry tree was an easy step.

I guess that just walking up and cutting it down all at once was a little too much for me, so I decided to *trim* it a little first. The result was that I left not a single limb intact. Our cherry tree was reduced to a forlorn-looking, tapering rod protruding from the ground. Around its base lay a pile of limbs with the leaves looking limp and sickly.

> *Blessed is the influence of one true loving human soul on another.*
> George Eliot

When I stepped back to survey my work, my conscience began. You know, consciences are often the most useless things. When I needed it was before I started, but it was completely silent then—didn't help me a lick. It never said, "John, you'd best think about this" or, "Are you sure this is what you want to do?" *Now*, when it was to late to be of any use whatsoever, here it came—full blast. "Now look what you've done," it cried. Pictures of my mother fertilizing and watering, her proud tones as she displayed those first cherries to all of her friends—all flooded my memory and made me feel terrible.

But what good did it do to feel terrible

after the fact?

It also occurred to me that this might not be easy to explain. I put my hatchet in its case and wandered slowly into the kitchen. I had studied some on how best to approach this situation and had decided that it would be to my best advantag᾽ to open the subject before it was discovered.

"I know a little boy who cut down a cherry tree," I piped in my most cheerful, winning voice.

My mother, busily occupied, laughed and replied, "Oh, I bet I know who it was. It was George Washington." She said it so nice and sweet that I was reassured and plunged ahead.

"No, it wasn't. It was John Smith."

Right off there was a noticeable change in both the temperature and the atmospheric pressure in the kitchen. My mother turned on me quickly, and her voice didn't have any sweetness to it.

"Did you cut down my cherry tree?" She grabbed me by my left ear (she was right-handed, so her grip was better), and we marched out to the scene of the crime—with her nearly lifting me off the ground, using my left ear for leverage.

I would have gone anyway.

When she saw the tree, she started to cry; and since she needed both hands to dry her eyes, she turned loose of my ear—which was a great relief. It was a sad-looking sight, standing there like a little flagpole—but I thought things might go a little easier for me since she was so sad and all. They didn't. She whipped me with every last limb I had chopped off that tree—whipped me till the limb was just shreds of bark left in her hand. I was afraid she was going to start on pear tree limbs, but she finally gave out. It cheered me some to think that she was using the *limbs* on me—

instead of the hatchet.

You know, my mother went right back to work on that cherry tree. She kept right on watering and fertilizing and caring for it. Anyone else would have given up. She willed that tree to live, and it did. It grew and became a fine tree, with only a few scars on its trunk—to remind me of my folly.

Love each other deeply,
because love covers
over a multitude of sins.

1 PETER 4:7–9

We are always too busy
for our children;
we never give them the time
or interest they deserve.
We lavish gifts upon them;
but the most precious gift ~
our personal association,
which means so much to
them ~ we give grudgingly.

MARK TWAIN

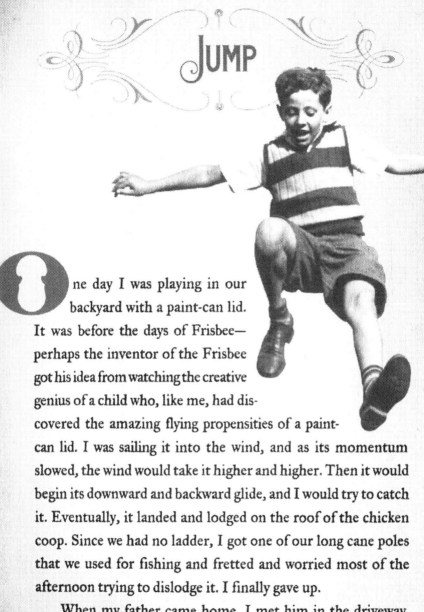

JUMP

One day I was playing in our backyard with a paint-can lid. It was before the days of Frisbee—perhaps the inventor of the Frisbee got his idea from watching the creative genius of a child who, like me, had discovered the amazing flying propensities of a paint-can lid. I was sailing it into the wind, and as its momentum slowed, the wind would take it higher and higher. Then it would begin its downward and backward glide, and I would try to catch it. Eventually, it landed and lodged on the roof of the chicken coop. Since we had no ladder, I got one of our long cane poles that we used for fishing and fretted and worried most of the afternoon trying to dislodge it. I finally gave up.

When my father came home, I met him in the driveway. Before he was out of the car, I began pleading with him to help me retrieve my toy. He put his lunch pail down on the front porch, and we walked around the house together. He assured me that it was no problem and that we could get it back.

He hoisted me up on his shoulders, then grabbed my feet and boosted me up onto the roof of the chicken coop. He told me to walk very carefully, because the coop was old and decaying. I retrieved my toy and returned to the edge of the coop. I felt very powerful looking down at my father. He smiled up at me and then held out his arms and said,

"Jump."

Even now—forty-five years later—I close my eyes, and I can see him, as plainly as I can see the lake and the trees from where I sit writing this just now. He was so tall, so strong, so confident—with his big, handsome, grinning face—that it is easier for me to imagine that day than the day he died.

I jumped. With no hesitation, I jumped, and he caught me easily and hugged me and then swung me to the ground. He sent me to fetch his lunch pail, and in a moment we were in the house and the incident was forgotten—

no, it wasn't forgotten, was it?

He would be amazed that I remember it—I'm sure that within a very short time, he forgot it. He

wasn't trying consciously to be a good father. He didn't come home that day with a plan to create a lasting memory for his son. It wasn't planned at all.

My point is that most parenting cannot be planned, except in your own personal walk with God and in prayer. Many great opportunities for lasting impressions are either lost or become negatives because

you can't fake what you are when the unexpected comes.

If my father had generally been selfishly unconcerned with his children's cares, there would have been no time or cause for him to turn this unexpected moment into a great triumph—he would have acted according to his nature, told me he was much too tired to fool with me, reprimanded me for my carelessness, and gone into the house, leaving me to my own devices—

and the moment would have been lost.

The opportunities come, and most of the time we react according to who we are rather that what we ought to be. We do not become good parents by trying to practice a parenting philosophy that is contrary to our natures. We become good parents—good neighbors, good husbands, and good friends—by becoming *good*—

by turning our lives toward God.

> *The best portion of a good man's life, is little, nameless, unremembered acts of kindness and of love.*
>
> WILLIAM WORDSWORTH

Train up a child
in the way
he should go,
and when he is old
he will not
turn from it.

Proverbs 22:6

———————————

The woman who
creates and sustains a home
and under whose hands
children grow up to be strong
and pure men and women,
is a creator second
only to God.

HELEN HUNT JACKSON

LEARNING TO READ

My mother taught me to read. She didn't mean to—I mean, she wasn't trying to—but she did. I don't know when she began to practice, but I do know that from my earliest remembrance, she read to me every day before I took my nap—except Saturday and Sunday. On weekdays my father would be at work and my sister at school, so we would crawl into my parents' bed and prop the pillows up against the iron posts of the bedstead—after fluffing them, of course. What a shame that modern children don't even know the word *fluffing*. They don't know it because they don't *fluff*—you can't with polyester and foam rubber. We've added *microchip* to our vocabulary and deleted *fluffing*. It was a sorry exchange, and our language is the more barren for it. Anyway, we would fluff the pillows, nestle back into them, huddle very close to each other, and she would read.

What did she read? The Bible, of course—what else? It was the only book in our house. She read stories from the Bible.

She was a finger reader.

Years later, when I went to school, I read the same way; but my teacher, Miss Smokey, absolutely forbade it. I told her my mother read that way, and she said it was OK for my mother, but not for me. Miss Smokey was very nice—and she meant well—but I'm really glad that my mother's teacher didn't forbid her to read with her finger, because, if she had, you see, I wouldn't have learned nearly so soon or so well, and I might not have loved it so.

Oh, you may not know what finger reading is. It's like fluffing, I guess. Finger reading is following the words with your finger so you won't lose your place or jump to the wrong line. It makes perfectly good sense if you think about it. In schools, nowadays, we're very concerned with how *fast* people read—if you can read a thousand words a minute, that is absolutely fantastic—and it really doesn't matter if you *understand* the words or *enjoy* them or take the time to *think* about them. You must learn to read them very quickly because there are so many of them, and if you don't read quickly—my goodness— you may never read all of them. And reading all of them is terribly important, even though many of them—

> *The mother's heart is the child's schoolroom.*
>
> HENRY WARD BEECHER

aren't worth much.

My mother was a finger reader. Every day as she read, I would hear her voice and watch her finger as it went back and forth across the page. Of course, it happened very slowly—and I didn't *know* I was learning to read. I honestly didn't mean to learn— it was quite an accident. Gradually, I began to associate what my mother was saying with the word above her finger. I guess I learned the *ands, thats,* and *buts* first—because there are so many of them—but it was easy for an uncluttered mind to grasp that it took a long time to say *Belshazzar* and that it also took a lot of letters, so I began to learn big words too. The more I learned, the more fascinated I became with my mother's voice and her moving finger.

One day I corrected her. She either mispronounced or skipped a word—I don't remember which—and I corrected her. She was incredulous. "How did you know that?" she asked. I didn't know how I knew; I just knew that the word she said wasn't the word that was above her finger. I didn't know the alphabet—that would come much later in school. I didn't know phonics—I still don't. But anybody who can tell the difference between a fire hydrant and a telephone pole can tell the difference between Jehu and Jerusalem. My mother asked me to read, and I did it gladly—slowly, haltingly—finger under the words. With her coaching, I read. Then I read with no coaching, and we took turns. Mom read one day; I read the next.

When I went to school a couple of years later, Miss Smokey tried to teach me to read. I told her I could already read. I could tell it hurt her feelings, so I said I was sorry—but reading was a piece of cake. They were reading Dick and Jane, and I knew Nebuchadnezzar, Jebusite, Perrizzzite, Shamgar, and Rehoboam. I told her she could teach me math—

I was real dumb in that.

But I want you to see that if my mother was teaching me to read— without meaning to—she was also teaching me about God, about right and wrong, about good and evil. Yes, those ideas were forming in my mind—waiting for the moment when I would need them to help me understand my growing, changing world.

She didn't mean to—any more than she meant to teach me to read. She read the Bible because she loved to read the Bible, because it had great meaning to her. If I hadn't been around, she would have read it anyway; and after I went to school and didn't take naps anymore, she continued to read. She only knew that it entertained me and that it was good for me in some general way.

Learning to read and learning about God—about good and evil and standing for the right—did not come to me through lectures and sermons, although I heard plenty of them at church. They came to me through my mother's attempt to establish and strengthen her own relationship with God.

Her daily awareness of His providence,
her constant devotion to Him
and to His Word passed to me—
naturally.

She speaks with wisdom,
and faithful instruction
is on her tongue. . . .
Her children arise
and call her blessed;
her husband also,
and he praises her.

PROVERBS 31:26–28

Just a song at twilight,
When the lights are low
And the flickering shadows
Softly come and go.
Tho' the heart be weary,
Sad the day and long,
Still to us at twilight
Comes Love's old sweet song.

G. CLIFTON BINGHAM

Love's Old Sweet Song

uring the year that we lived on Gardenia Street in Royal Oak, I got very sick. I think it was some sort of influenza, but our family didn't go to the doctor much, so we never knew. We accepted our sicknesses as a part of God's divine providence, and we worked our way through them as best we could. We cured everything with chicken noodle soup, dry toast, poached eggs, and hot tea. (I highly recommend this remedy to all parents; it has the advantage of not only working but being very cheap.)

I had been sick for several days, and my vomiting, fever, and inability to eat or drink had made me very weak. My mother had stayed at my bedside or close-by the entire time. My dad was working at some kind of tool and die shop, so I only saw him in the

evenings. When he came home, he would stick his head in the door to see if I was awake. If I was, he'd grin real big and say, "Hey, Bud, how're you doing? You feel like going fishing?" He said it so cheerfully that it made me feel better.

That was at first.

Toward the end, when I was so sick and weak that I could scarcely speak and they had begun to worry, he'd come in and take my hand or rumple my hair a little, and he'd say, "How you feeling, Son? Is there anything I can do for you?" His face would be filled with care, and I was sorry to worry him so.

One night, very late, I awoke slowly from my feverish sleep. The light was on in the hallway, and the door to my room was open just a crack. In the shadowy half-light, I could see someone sitting by my bed. I thought it was my mother. I must have moved a little because I felt someone squeeze my hand. I knew it wasn't my mother. The hand was large, strong, and rough. Without turning my head, I moved my eyes slowly in his direction. My dad was sitting, slumped over in a chair. He still had on his work clothes—a light blue shirt and dark blue pants, with heavy black shoes and white socks. There were stains on the shirt, and it smelled that kind of burnt-oil smell that saturated all his shop uniforms. His head was resting in his free hand, his eyes were closed, and there were tears on his face. When I saw his lips move a little—

I knew immediately that he was praying.

My dad was singing "Love's Old Sweet Song"—not those words and not the music, you understand—but the oldest, sweetest song there is. A song that has been sung since the beginning of time. When my heart is weary—"sad the day and long"—at twilight I remember those days and love's old sweet song. My dad was singing it at its very best.

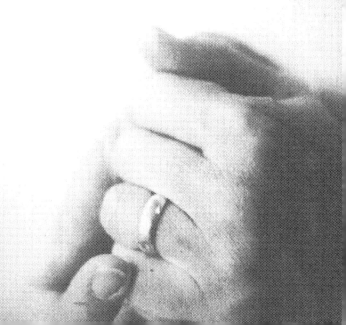

The door of prayer
has been open
ever since God
made man
in his own image.

GEORGE MACDONALD

A kind heart is
a fountain of gladness,
making everything
in its vicinity
freshen into smiles.

WASHINGTON IRVING

My Mother Played the Piano

My mother played the piano. She played mostly by ear, I think, but she often looked at the notes too. She played "Red River Valley," "When My Blue Moon Turns to Gold Again," and "Mexicali Rose"—but mostly she played church songs.

As I remember, she mostly played in the early or midafternoon. During the summer months, I would approach our little white house, and through the open windows with the white curtains moving with the breeze, I would hear her playing and singing. It was a very comforting, reassuring sound. I'm sure it brought much happiness to her.

Sometimes when I came in to get a drink or some needed thing or to ask if I could go farther than normal, she would say, "John, come here and sing this with me." She didn't say it like a command or an order or anything like that—not like when she said, "Go clean the chicken coop" or, "Go hoe the garden." Those were orders. She would just say it like a request or like she would appreciate it as a favor.

I usually didn't want to. I was afraid my friends would hear through the open window—or worse yet, that they would ask, "What took you so long?" and I would have to say, "I was singing some church songs with my mother," and I could just imagine the looks they would give me—like my driveway didn't go all the way to the street or something.

I made every possible excuse I could. Of course, I didn't just say no. You can't do that with requests, you know; and besides, I didn't say that word to my parents. The "no" word was the death word, and if I said it—even in fun—I would die.

I always knew that.

"Come on, John," she would coax. "It will only take a minute."

"Oh, Mom," I would say. "Oh, *Mother*"—the exasperation and disgust would absolutely drip from my voice, but usually I would go, dragging my reluctant feet to her.

She would be so enthusiastic. She would say, "Now, I want you to sing this alto part for me." And she would play it and sing it, and then she would play it while I sang it. Then she would play the soprano part and sing that, and then she would play both of them and sing my part. Then she would play both parts, and I would sing alto while she sang soprano. You can't imagine how excited she would be when we finished. "Isn't that the prettiest song you ever heard?" she would exclaim. If I thought it was something less than that—

I certainly kept it to myself.

I played my role halfheartedly at best. But sometimes I just couldn't get into it at all and sang so poorly and was so sour-faced and sullen that she would slowly close the book, pat me on the shoulder, and say, "You go on back to your friends, now. We'll do this some other time."

Although I was a reluctant participant, the memories of playing the piano with my mother are among my sweetest. Sometimes now, when I can find a place where it is still and allow myself to be

> *Of all the music that reached farthest into heaven, it is the beating of a loving heart.*
>
> HENRY WARD BEECHER

very quiet, I can see the old white house with the white curtains moving at the open windows. And through those open windows, I hear her voice and see those nimble fingers moving on the keys.

"From this valley they say you are going,
we will miss your bright eyes and sweet smile,
for they say you are taking the sunshine
that has brightened our path for a while."

"Come on, John," she coaxes.
"It will only take a minute.
You sing the alto—it goes like this—
and I'll sing soprano.
Isn't that the most beautiful song you ever heard?"

And in my mind I say, "I'm coming, Mom," and I rush to her with joy because I know how happy it will make her.

And it is, you know,
the most beautiful song
I've ever heard.

For when you looked
into my mother's eyes
you knew,
as if He had told you,
why God sent her
into the world ~
it was to open the minds
of all who looked,
to beautiful thoughts.

Sir James M. Barrie

So I commend
the enjoyment of life. . . .
Then joy will
accompany him
in his work all the days
of the life
God has given him
under the sun.

ECCLESIASTES 8:15

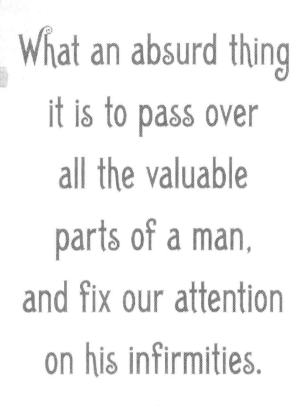

What an absurd thing
it is to pass over
all the valuable
parts of a man,
and fix our attention
on his infirmities.

Joseph ADDISON

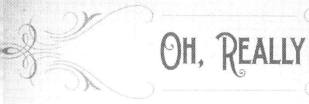

OH, REALLY

We moved from Allen Park, Michigan, back to Royal Oak when I was a sophomore in high school. I didn't know too many people there, but I struck up a tentative friendship with a boy who sang first tenor next to me in the a cappella choir. One day we were talking before practice began—that inquisitive, casual but probing kind of talk that ultimately determines whether your friendship rises or falls. He told me where his father worked and what an important position he held. I told him that my dad sold batteries and electrical parts for cars.

He asked if I was familiar with a certain ladies' fashion store in town. When I said I had heard of it, he said—

with an air of unconcealed pride—that his mother owned that store and was responsible for its operation. Not to be outdone, I quickly related that my mother worked for Judge Arthur E. Moore. When he asked what she did, I said she was a housekeeper. He was obviously impressed by the name, but he was uncertain about the term "housekeeper." When he inquired as to what a housekeeper did, I said that she cooked, cleaned, made beds, and did laundry for them.

"You mean your mother is a *cleaning lady?*" His tone was slightly incredulous.

I said that I guessed that was right, but I had never thought about it exactly in those terms.

He turned to the boy sitting beside him and said, "Hey, John's mother is a *cleaning lady.*"

"Oh, really," the boy responded. There was no mistaking the tone.

For the first time in my life, I wished my mother had a different job.

It bothered me all day. It occurred to me on my way home that I had never thought of my mother as a *cleaning lady.* I thought of her, more than anything, as my mother. I thought of her work as being very necessary and useful— much more useful than a fashion shop, when it came down to it. I decided that a person needed to know much more about my mother and her work before they were qualified to say, "Oh, really."

It was obvious to me, even then, that my friendship with those boys was going to be very limited because of my parents' occupations. I am very sorry to say that I felt the loss deeply. I had no way of knowing then that their friendship was worth about what a ladies' fashion shop is worth—almost nothing. I was ashamed of my mother's job and never, ever mentioned it again to anyone, but it didn't help. There were too many other unmistakable signs about me—signs I didn't even know about and couldn't possibly cover up. I was classified. Son of a Cleaning Lady was the sign I wore. And instead of accepting it with dignity, I languished under its reproach.

It hurts me now to think that I was ever ashamed of my mother or anything about her. I know that children— especially from junior high through college—often are ashamed or embarrassed by some things about their parents. If they have unimportant jobs, if they wear outdated, nerdy clothes, if they are much overweight, if they have old-fashioned ideas about music or morals

or movies, if they drive the wrong cars or are just out of touch—kids have a tendency to avoid bringing friends home and often don't want their parents to attend school functions.

Children must be taught to look deeper—to see beyond those transitory, surface evaluations of worth. Parents must not demean other people in their children's presence on such a shallow basis. When your children hear you speak of others, do you sometimes say,

"Oh, really"?

By loving whatever is
lovable in those around us,
love will flow back from them
to us, and life will become
a pleasure instead of a pain;
and earth will
become like Heaven;
and we shall become
not unworthy followers
of Him whose name is Love.

A. P. Stanley

Do nothing
out of selfish ambition
or vain conceit,
but in humility
consider others better
than yourselves.

Ephesians 2:3

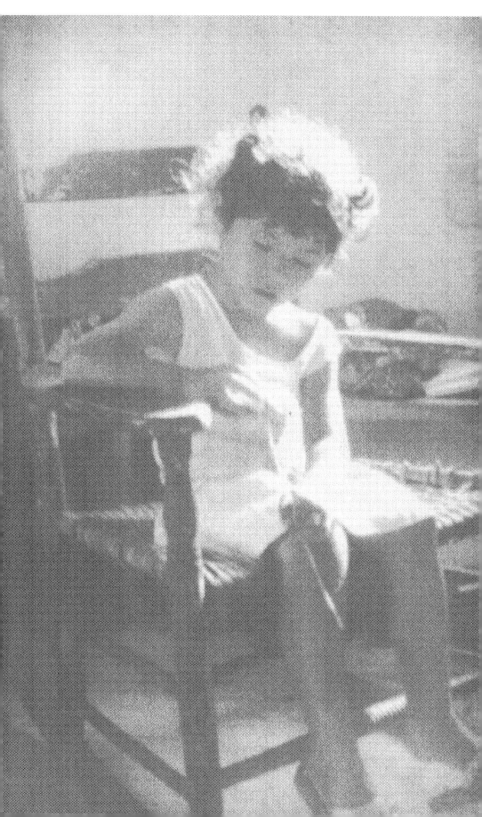

Life is a
constant becoming:
all stages lead
to the beginning
of others.

GEORGE BERNARD SHAW

THE UPWARD WAY

The boy was short, and he still had quite a bit of "baby fat." He wore glasses, and he was often teased. His school record was far from brilliant, except that his teachers favored him because he was well mannered and said "sir" and "ma'am." His father and mother were concerned because he had no victories. He never won anything. He didn't make any of the teams, and he wasn't a brilliant student. He lacked aggressiveness, and he seemed to

be constantly withdrawn. He had little enthusiasm for life—

and he was alone much.

Behind their house were some high mountains topped by great, jagged upthrusts of perpendicular rock. The steep slopes beneath were extremely rugged and forbidding and were covered with pin-oak brush, cat's-claw, cactus, manzanita, ironwood, and ponderosa pine—with an occasional blue spruce. The washes, which carried the spring runoff, cut deep ravines in these slopes. They were choked with huge boulders that had fallen ages ago and with fallen trees, brush, and other debris. The father noticed that the boy looked often toward those craggy summits, gazing in wonder at their majesty.

One winter day, when the sun was glistening radiantly from the snow-covered peaks, the boy expressed his desire to someday climb to the top. The father determined that his chance would come.

Accordingly, one fine spring day—with no warning—the father announced that there would be no school that day. A special project was planned. The anticipation—as they filled canteens, packed a lunch, and dressed appropriately in climbing clothes—lit the boy's face and put a fire in his eyes that the father had rarely seen. They drove their four-wheel-drive truck up the

> *Good actions are the invisible hinges on the doors of heaven.*
>
> VICTOR HUGO

mountain as far as the last rut-riddled road would take them, found a promising ravine, and set out.

Those who mounted Everest worked no harder, suffered no greater hardship or discouragement, and had no greater desire to quit. The father had not realized how difficult a task he had set, but he knew they must not fail; the boy must accomplish this. The boy—red-faced from exertion, panting hoarsely, sweating profusely—hinted more than once that perhaps they ought to return.

But the heroic ascent continued.

Finally, they broke out into the open, and the panorama of the miles they could see was awesome. Their whole town, tucked away in a fold of lesser hills, looked insignificant. "I'll bet we can see Flagstaff from the top," the boy cried, and they plunged ahead.

When they came to a second opening, they stopped and ate part of their lunch. They rested their weary backs and aching legs against a great ponderosa. They shared a tree, a sandwich, a canteen, a view, a struggle, a hope, their fatigue, and they shared the marvelous silence.

"It sure is quiet, isn't it, Dad?" the boy whispered. "I never heard it so quiet before."

They were close, and it was good.

There was no talk of returning now. When they finally, reluctantly—but with renewed vigor—left their lunch spot, they only talked of how long, how far to the top. The last seventy-five yards was hand-over-hand climbing up a nearly vertical, rock-ribbed surface. As they neared the top, their hearts were pounding, and they were absolutely breathless. The father came behind—to help the boy, to reassure him against falling, and because he wanted him to be first. When the boy finally topped the ascent, he paused and turned, his long brown hair moving with the wind. He stretched out his hands and said,

"Let me help you up, Dad. It's great."

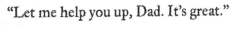

Nothing great
was ever achieved
without enthusiasm.

RALPH WALDO EMERSON

I have fought
the good fight,
I have finished
the race,
I have kept
the faith.

2 TIMOTHY 4:7

———————

The only faith
that wears well and
holds its color in all weather
is that which is
woven of conviction.

James Russell Lowell

WHICH KIND ARE YOU?

One night after church, Judi needed a few things from the store, and because it was totally dark and raining lightly, I dropped her off at the front door. I parked where I could see both store exits so that when she came out, I could pick her up. For this time of night, there were a lot of shoppers. I opened my window about three inches to keep it from fogging.

There was a Chevy station wagon parked pretty close to me, and as I waited, the family who owned it came out. They had their sacks of groceries in a shopping cart.

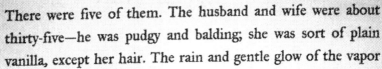

There were five of them. The husband and wife were about thirty-five—he was pudgy and balding; she was sort of plain vanilla, except her hair. The rain and gentle glow of the vapor lights in the parking lot caused it to shine nice and soft, and it curled all over her head and neck and down onto her face. I wanted to tell her how pretty it was, but I didn't. They had a boy—about ten, I guess. He was pushing the cart. He looked about right—jeans, T-shirt, and Reeboks. There were two nondescript others—about four and six, maybe, but their gender will forever remain a mystery.

The father opened the tailgate of the station wagon, and he and the boy unloaded the cart. When they finished, the father said, "Run the cart over there to the collection area, Danny."

As I said, it was raining—not hard, though. The rain wasn't offensive, just sort of a warm, pleasant drizzle that makes you want a good book, a fire, someone you love, and the leisure to be drowsy.

The boy didn't want to do it. They were about forty yards from me. I could hear them plainly, but I'm sure they never noticed me.

"Aw, Dad, it's raining," he complained.

"It will only take a second, and it won't

hurt you." But there was no conviction in his voice. The father was reasoning with the boy—treating him as an equal— and the boy took full advantage.

"Those people over there didn't put theirs back," he argued, pointing to the several carts carelessly left in various places.

"We're not responsible for them, just for us," the father rejoined.

"But who cares?" the boy replied. "They hire people to come out here and collect these carts."

The mother, tired of waiting, now joined in on the boy's side. "For heaven's sake, Carl, come on! One more cart in the parking lot won't change the history of the world."

The boy sensed victory. He quickly pushed the cart to one side and opened the door to get in. The father shrugged his shoulders in defeat, moved to the driver's door, and put his hand on the handle. Then he stopped. At first I couldn't figure out why, but I followed his eyes across the misty

> *All that is necessary for the triumph of evil is that good men do nothing.*
>
> EDMUND BURKE

parking lot, and I saw what he saw—an elderly couple, her arm in his, slowly pushing their cart toward the collection area. It caused a whole transformation in him. His posture straightened, his chin lifted, and his shoulders squared a little. I suspect he looked much like the man he had been when he got married. And when he spoke, there was firmness and authority in his voice. "Danny," he said, "come here."

Danny didn't *hesitate*, and Danny didn't *argue*—
Danny came.

"Do you see those carts that are in the cart collection area? There are two kinds of people, Danny: those who put their carts away and those who don't. In this family we put our carts away, because that's the kind of people we are. Don't ever forget that, Danny. Now put that cart where it belongs."

As the boy directed the cart to its appropriate place, it occurred to me how right the father was. There are two kinds of people in every area of life—and two kinds of fathers.

Which kind are you?

What a father
says to his children
is not heard
by the world,
but it will be heard
by posterity.

JEAN PAUL RICHTER

Do not merely
listen to the word,
and so deceive
yourselves.
Do what it says.

JAMES 1:22

PART TWO

Childhood Memories

An open foe
may prove a curse;
but a
pretended friend
is worse.

BENJAMIN FRANKLIN

THE NEIGHBORHOOD MOOCHERS

About two months ago, I was talking to a close relative of mine who still lives in the same area of Michigan where I was raised; he goes to church where my parents and I went. He asked me if I remembered a lady named

Norma who had lived right down the street from them. It took me a moment to respond, because I remembered her all too well, but I finally managed a weak affirmation. He said that she had died a week or two earlier.

I was sorry to hear it. Norma played a very important role in my growing up. She didn't plan to; God just providentially used her for that purpose. I suppose that since both she and my parents are gone, I ought to tell this story for my children and for yours. Although it is very embarrassing to me, I can tell it with a good heart, and no one can be hurt by it but me.

When I was twelve, our family finances got so bad that we moved into a cabin in an old trailer park at the corner of Twelve Mile Road and Crooks Road. Originally these cabins had been built as the precursors of motels—as a place for travelers to spend the night. As the town had spread out around them and travelers no longer came that way, the cabins fell into disuse, so the owners decided to rent them out by the month. My dad operated a Standard Oil gas station right across the street, so it was a convenient place to live.

I soon made friends with another boy in the trailer park named Don. In most ways we had little in common. We were drawn together by our age, our physical proximity, our mutual poverty, and our love for baseball.

We were baseball fanatics. We played at every opportunity, and when we couldn't find a game, we played catch in the trailer park. When dark came, we would play catch near the office lights of the trailer park until the residents got tired of the noise of the ball splatting in our gloves and drove us off. Then we would go and peruse our baseball cards. We had hundreds of them. We knew the names, positions, batting averages, and ERAs of every Detroit Tiger.

When the neighborhood kids played, it was sort of understood that we would take turns supplying a ball. Don and I never did supply because we never had a decent ball, and our friends constantly reminded us of the fact. They called us the

neighborhood moochers.

When we showed up to play, they would say, "Here come the neighborhood moochers." For those of you who may not know the word *moocher*—it's another way of calling a person a bum or beggar.

Don and I would go to the high-school field and spend long hours on Saturday looking for stray balls. The ones we found were always in sorry condition. The stitches were frayed or loose, and the covers were torn. We tried to hide a multitude of sins with black electrical tape, but the results were very dissatisfying.

We began to talk about how great it would be to see the looks on our friends' faces if we showed up with a brand-new ball—especially a *Reach*. That was the kind the Tigers played with. They had them at Montgomery Ward, but they were $2.75 and might as well have been $100. But we couldn't get it out of our minds or our conversation. We didn't like to be called *bums* or *moochers* by our friends. We would walk to Royal Oak and go to Montgomery Ward to look at the baseballs. We would pick up the display model and lovingly caress the smooth, white horsehide cover, finger the flawless red stitching, admire the dark blue "Reach" printed on the side, and imagine ourselves hitting home runs and throwing blazing fast balls.

It would not have occurred to me to steal one—
at least not seriously.

My home life and religious training had created inhibitions far too deep for that. But Don was not religious, and the only reservations he had were limited to the possibilities of getting caught. He mentioned it often. I would not consider it. Then he made a suggestion that allowed me to rationalize my reserves. He said that he would actually steal the ball; I would only divert the sales clerk. I thought that I could do that, so I went along—

but I knew better.

I did my job. I diverted the sales clerk by pretending to be interested in some article far away from the baseballs. Don had on a jacket, and he slipped the ball underneath his jacket and under his armpit and walked out of the store. In a couple of minutes, I followed. As I made my way up the stairs, I heard a familiar female voice call my name. I turned, and there stood Norma, a lady who went to church with us.

She asked me to come back down and talk to her. I didn't want to, but I went. She asked me what I was doing at the store. I was so flustered and nervous that I couldn't say anything. She told me that she was a store detective and that she had seen Don take the baseball and knew that I had helped him. I tried at first to explain the harmlessness of my involvement, but it was no use—I was just as guilty as Don—

and we both knew it.

There are no words to adequately describe all the feelings that poured over me in a moment of time—what this would mean to my family, the church, my friends. She told me to go and get Don and to bring him and the ball back.

He was standing outside, flushed with excitement because we had *gotten away with it*. When I told him we hadn't, he wanted to run. He said no one could catch us, but

I knew there was no place
for me to run to.

I told him we had to go back. He wouldn't go—but he gave me the ball and said I could go back if I wanted to, and he took off.

Like a sheep to the slaughter, I went back. I told Norma that Don had run away. She said that she didn't care about him, but she just couldn't understand how I could do such a thing. *I didn't really understand it either.* We talked for along time, and I cried— she did too. I wondered what she was going to do with me.

When we finished talking, she just sat sort of hunched over with her chin resting in her hand. She looked at me for a long time—like she was having trouble making up her mind. She finally straightened up and sighed—a great big, long one, like she had been holding her breath for about ten minutes—which let me know she had made up her mind. She reached out and took me by my chin. She held my face right up to hers and made me look straight into her eyes, and she said,

"Johnny, you go home,
and don't you ever let me catch you
in this store without your parents
ever again.
This will stay be
tween the two of us."

I don't remember every going back into Montgomery Ward ever again—not even with my parents.

The LORD
detests lying lips,
but he delights
in men who
are truthful.

Proverbs 12:22

When it comes to life,
the critical thing
is whether you
take things for granted
or take them
with gratitude.

G. K. CHESTERTON

RUBBER ICE

It was late February or early March, and James and I were playing at the gravel pit. It was a cold, windy, overcast day, with a few flakes of snow flying, but we were having a great time. I had on my first pair of genuine boots—rubber footwear that you could actually stick your foot right down into with no shoes on, and you didn't have to buckle them. They were black with red soles and a little too large for me. (My mother had bought them at a sale, and neither size nor comfort was a major consideration.) Even with two pairs of socks, I "clumped" in them considerably. They came almost to my knees and looked like firemen's boots.

I was exceedingly proud of them.

There was a patch of thin ice at the edge of the gravel pit, and we were breaking that ice by stomping on it and then splashing through into the shallow water beneath it. I had been doing this for some time when I found a small pool, covered with what we called "rubber ice." It was not actually part of the gravel pit, but it was connected by a narrow neck of water. The ice would actually give with your weight and then spring back—a sort of trampoline effect. You can imagine what fun I had with it. Suddenly, it gave way, and I fell into some sandy water unlike any I had ever been in before. I sank immediately over my boots up to my thighs. Terrified, I began to struggle, but I simply could not extricate myself. This produced a fear that resulted in an absolute frenzy of effort to get out. The only noticeable result was that I was nearly up to my armpits within a minute or so.

I did not know that I should remain calm—I simply wore myself out struggling. Finally, I had no energy left, and the absolute futility of further efforts overwhelmed me. James heard my cries and came to help me, but he quickly realized that he could be of no assistance. He stood completely helpless, within ten feet of me. As I grew calmer, I noticed that I wasn't sinking as fast. I told James to run and get Elmer Russell. He was a well driller, and I knew he was home because I had spoken to him on my way to the gravel pit.

When they returned a few minutes later, I had sunk past my armpits. I was numb from the effect of the freezing sand and water and was quite concerned about my condition. Elmer had brought a rope. He got a circle of it over my head, and I grabbed it with my hands. Being an extremely powerful man, he pulled me out with relative ease. Unfortunately, he pulled me right out of my boots. It was about a mile or so to my house, but I ran all the way—

in my socks.

I thought I would receive the whipping of my life, but you know, the funniest thing happened. When my mother first saw me—soaking wet, mud and sand right up to my ears, my boots gone—she was real upset. I tried to tell her what had happened, but it was a less-than-convincing story. Just about the time I finished my explanation, the phone rang, and it was Elmer Russell calling to see if I had gotten home all right. He talked to my mom—

for a long time.

When she hung up, there were great tears in her eyes, and she came and hugged me and kissed me. She helped me undress, got the washtub, heated some water, and made me take a hot bath—it wasn't even Saturday!—gave me some hot tea, and put me to bed. I couldn't make any sense out of it at all. When my father came home that evening, I thought sure I was going to catch it good.

For some reason my parents went to their bedroom to talk, which was really unusual, because normally when I messed up, they talked right in front of me—so I would know what was coming, I guess. I heard her say, "Oh, Fred, Elmer told me that another five minutes and he would have been gone. *We almost lost him*." When my dad came out, he didn't say much, but I noticed that when we prayed at supper that night, he mentioned me several times and told God how grateful he was that He looked after me when he couldn't.

On Sunday afternoon my father and I walked over to the

gravel pit, and I showed him the place—I guess he wanted to look for my boots, but they were nowhere in sight. He stood there by the little pond of water a long time and looked. Again he didn't say much, but I thought I noticed him wiping his eyes a time or two with the back of his hand, and I wondered about it, because the wind was hardly blowing—

and it wasn't that cold.

P.S. Late that fall I was playing at the gravel pit one sunny afternoon with James (I told you I wasn't real bright as a youngster—some might argue that age hasn't helped substantially), and we found one of my boots sticking right up out of the ground. I pulled it out and took it home, but it wasn't much good. I always wondered what happened to the other one.

We never
know the worth
of water
till the well
is dry.

OLD ENGLISH PROVERB

The LORD is good
and his love
endures forever;
his faithfulness
continues through
all generations.

Psalm 100:5

Do not keep the alabaster
boxes of your love and
tenderness sealed up until
your friends are dead.
Fill their lives with sweetness.
Speak approving
cheering words while
their ears can hear them and
while their hearts can be
thrilled by them.

HENRY WARD BEECHER

INNOCENCE LOST

Picture a street . . . ah, no, picture two streets running parallel. Between those two streets is an alley. On either side of this alley, facing opposite directions, are two rows of houses. Have you got that? Now here's the hard part. One of the houses is missing. That space, where the house is missing, is called a vacant lot—because, dearly beloved—

it has no house.

This vacant lot had become a playground for all the neighborhood children. Tag, hide-and-seek, kick-the-can, fox-and-goose, and yes, even the national pastime—baseball—were all played upon this lot.

One fine, fall afternoon, about ten boys were gathered for a baseball game. They ranged in age from nine to thirteen. They wore old, black sneakers or were barefoot.

Their T-shirts were dirty from the day's play, and their blue jeans (either it was before the advent of Levi's or we couldn't afford them) were worn, patched, or out at the knees. Their equipment consisted of a single baseball, whose cover had long since disappeared and been replaced by black electrical tape wound carefully round and round the strings of the ball. There was one bat—it was broken. It had three wood screws holding it together, and it, too, was taped. The bases were either newspapers or rags held in place by rocks. Since there was no first baseman or right fielder, the pitcher could get a first-base runner out from the pitcher's mound, and any ball hit to right field was an automatic out.

The game was hotly contested; the lead had seesawed back and forth. No major-league contest was ever played with more intensity. I was pitching. My friend David Moody, a year and a half younger than I, was on the other team. David was not a very good player, and he was at bat.

He hadn't been on base all day. He had struck out, popped up, hit to right field, or had found some new, creative way to make an out. As I said, he was my friend. We had grown up together. His folks and mine had gone to church together time out of mind. They even went to dinner and played pinochle together. His older sisters, Audrey and Faye, were my sister's best friends.

Although the game was close, my team was ahead and I felt very benevolent toward David. I gave him a nice, soft pitch right down the middle. David promptly took advantage of my kindness and smacked the ball across the street into Mrs. Owen's rose bushes. He got all the way to second base. Maybe that's where the trouble started. I was miffed because

he had taken advantage of my generosity.

A couple of plays later, another boy got a hit, and David decided to further impress his teammates and score. It was a mistake. He was a very slow runner. My job as pitcher was to cover home plate. I had the ball, waiting to tag him out, fifteen feet before he ever got there. He knew he didn't stand a chance, but he decided to try the only option left to him. He charged me—which was another mistake. I was a whole head taller, thirty pounds heavier, and I saw him coming. Like I said, I guess it started when he hit my pitch so hard. I had the ball in my glove, and when he dove at me, headfirst, I just stepped back; and as he flew by, I hit him right in the face with my glove.

It sort of stunned him at first, but I could tell he was real upset. Everybody making fun of him didn't help, but then he made another mistake—worse than the first two. He decided to fight. I just made fun of it at first. When he tried to hit me, I just ducked or warded off his blows. He really got mad then. I guess he sort of went crazy, and I couldn't stop him from hitting me, and I started to get upset myself. I pleaded with him to stop, but he was like a human tornado. Finally, he hit me right on my ear, and I got mad—really mad. I hit him on the nose and knocked him down. Then I jumped on him, pinned his arms to the ground with my knees, and proceeded to slap his face with my open hand. Back and forth—back of my hand,

palm of my hand—I slapped him. The other boys had made a circle around us and were yelling encouragement to both of us—

which wasn't help to either of us.

When I began to come to myself, when the light of reason began to filter through my red brain, I looked down and saw the face of my friend, David Moody. It was covered with blood from his nose and mouth. I was absolutely horrified by what I was doing. It was against everything I had ever been taught. I was not by nature a bully and normally avoided fights of any kind. I didn't even like to watch.

I jumped up, and I began to run. I raced down the alley into an intersecting alley, down it to the street, across the street, and into another vacant lot, which was across from my house. I was so overcome by the course of events that I knelt there and began to cry.

I hadn't even realized that David was following me. Still angry, bent on vengeance, he came to where I was and found me kneeling and crying. He stood behind me a moment, then stooped down and put his arms around me, and he, too, began to cry.

Picture it if you will, two boys—one eleven, the other thirteen—arms around each other, crying in a vacant lot from their first real, dawning consciousness of wrongdoing—

     of having violated some sacred injunction.

True to our teaching, our heritage, we begged forgiveness of each other. We made a pact, as boys will, to ever be friends and to never allow anything to separate us. The pact worked. We never fought again or even had cross words. I'm sorry to say that it wasn't due to our fidelity or our characters. David Moody died about a month later in a drowning accident. I remember his funeral, and I remember thinking when the preacher was talking that he didn't know David very well. I wished they would have let me talk because I could have told them something that would have made their hearts glad.

I rejoice today that David and I parted forgiven.

Pleasant words
are a honeycomb,
sweet to the soul
and healing
to the bones.

Proverbs 16:24

Do all the good you can,
By all the means you can,
In all the ways you can,
To all the people you can,
As long as ever you can.

JOHN WESLEY

FEELING SORRY FOR ALEC

Alec Redmon lived on Rochester Road, about a half-mile from me. I had to pass his house on my way to school and on my way home. Alec was a bully. He had been held back in school, and he was older, taller, and stronger than the rest of us. He had threatened me, shoved me around, knocked my books out of my hands, and knocked my hat off. He had baited and provoked me in every conceivable way—taunting and heckling and knowing that I dared not challenge his vastly superior size and strength. I was terrified of him. What he did to me physically was absolutely nothing compared to the mental anguish—the anxiety produced by my imagination every morning and afternoon.

In order to avoid him, I went blocks out of my way, taking long detours and varying my route so he would never

know exactly which way I had gone. But one afternoon I forgot about Alec. I was so preoccupied with whatever I was pursuing that I did not take any of my detours. I was not aware of my mistake until I was shaken from my reverie by the sound of Alec's voice calling my name.

I stopped dead in my tracks, my heart beating wildly, my mind racing, my mouth suddenly dry, and with a nauseating sickness in my stomach. He ran across the road—right up to me—and I prepared for the worst.

He said, "Hey, John, we got that big test in history tomorrow, and you're pretty good in there. Would you come over tonight and help me study?"

I was stunned, absolutely speechless—the thought of Alec needing my help with anything was beyond my comprehension. Alec, obviously thinking that I would refuse, began to apologize for all of his meanness. He paused, looking down, and he said quietly, "I'm really sorry for all the mean things I've done to you. I don't know why I do them, and sometimes, afterward, I hate myself. John, I really need some help. If I fail that test, I'm going to be held back again."

"I guess I could do that," I mumbled.

"Thanks, John; it would mean a lot to me. Thanks a lot."

I went home very thoughtfully, not at all sure I had done the right thing. When I asked my mother for permission to go over to Alec's house, she said, "Isn't that the boy you've had so much trouble with?"

"Yes, ma'am."

"Do you think it's wise to go over there?"

I told my mother what had happened that afternoon, and she told me that I was doing exactly what Jesus would do. That made me feel better, but you need to know that my walk to the Redmons' house that night was one of the most daring and brave things I have ever done. Many things in my later life, which might appear to have required courage, pale into insignificance in comparison to what it took to keep going that night.

Many are the plans in a man's heart, but it is the LORD'S purpose that prevails.

PROVERBS 19:21

The Redmons had their porch light on, and Mrs. Redmon met me at the door. I had never thought of Alec Redmon having a mother—it seemed incongruous. Somehow the fact that he had one was reassuring. She was a very nice lady, and she thanked me over and over for coming to help Alec. The Redmon house was much larger than ours, but it smelled about the same. All houses and families have a smell, you know—that's how dogs know their owners. You get so used to your own smell that you don't notice it, but you sure notice other people's smells because they're different. The Redmons' house smelled different, but not much—

and it wasn't a bad difference.

Alec and I went up to his room to study. I could tell you a lot about his room, but it's enough to say that it was pretty much like mine.

What I found out, studying with Alec, was that *he couldn't read*. I couldn't believe it—I mean, reading was the easiest thing in the world, and it was fun too. *Alec couldn't read*, not even the simple stuff. As I read to him and explained what the words meant and tried to help him understand about the Civil War and how it affected our country, something happened. It was not a conscious thought, but somehow, even then, I knew I would never, ever be afraid of Alec Redmon again. How could I be afraid of someone who couldn't read? I felt sorry for Alec.

Imagine that—me feeling sorry for Alec.

I could add that Alec and I became friends—pretty good friends—and remained friends until I moved away. I also need to say that my faith in goodness had been restored. Oh, it has been refined and expanded, but it is much the same now as it was when I was a child.

Goodness *will prevail*. Make no mistake about it. There is an absolute power and safety in goodness that evil cannot overcome.

Do not be afraid to align yourself with goodness.

The victories of evil are short-lived
and self-destructive.
Goodness will prevail.

The greatest thing
a person can do
for his heavenly Father
is to be kind
to some of God's
other children.

HENRY DRUMMOND

Make sure that
nobody pays back
wrong for wrong,
but always try
to be kind to each other
and to everyone else.

1 Thessalonians 5:15

The real voyage
of discovery consists
not in seeking
new landscapes,
but in having
new eyes.

MARCEL PROUST

Where Did It Go?

She really didn't want to go, but she had taken the boy to the holiday pageant because she wanted to be a good mother. It was about what she'd expected—poorly done, old costumes, missed lines, a hackneyed repeat of familiar words and tunes, with the characters played by less than amateurs. The boy had been fascinated by *the star*. It was the only really well-done piece in the set. Someone had obviously put some time, experience, and thought into it. It revolved high above the stage, sparkling and twinkling, constantly bringing back even an unwilling gaze. The boy had asked what it was, and she had given the old, stock answer. She was relieved when it was finally over.

It was dark when they left, very dark, and very cold, but it was marvelously clear. She hurried toward the car and regretted that she'd had to park so far away. She kept his hand in hers, and when he stumbled, she almost fell with him.

"Watch where you're going," she said—perhaps more crossly than she intended. She stopped to help him to his feet.

"I was looking for the star," he said apologetically.

"Why, there are millions of them," she misunderstood.

"I was looking for *His* star," he corrected.

"Oh, don't be silly, honey. That was just a play. The star went away long ago. You can't see it anymore."

"Where did it go? How do you know you can't see it anymore?" He was disappointed but continued to look.

"I don't know where it went, honey; it just went away, and that's why you can't see it. Come on now; we've got to hurry."

"Maybe it's that one!" He pointed to a particularly bright, friendly star.

"Is that Jesus's star?"

"No, honey, it's not Jesus's star. It's just a bright star."

"But it *could* be His star," he insisted. "Maybe it's come back."

Across her consciousness there flashed a *thought*. Where it came from, who could guess? Some might say that the spirit, ever watchful, never sleeping, seized this precious moment when her guard was down and kindled into flame a thought, a thought that had lain dormant for years.

"Oh, God," she thought, "I wish it were His star; I wish it had come back—

I wish I could believe in it like I used to."

She did not say it aloud, but it was there—and then it was blotted out by cold, fatigue, and pressing cares—but not completely. It was a prayer, and it was heard in the heart of Him who hears the beating of our hearts and knows our every thought—and who waits for moments like these to work His will in our lives. Before she had thought of what to say to her son, His messengers were speeding faster than light to respond.

> Be honest and
> fair with
> [children];
> be just; be tender;
> and they will
> make you rich
> in love and joy.
>
> ROBERT INGERSOLL

At the boy's insistence, she finally looked up, and there was a star! I mean, it was as different from other stars as a bonfire is from a kitchen match. She glanced quickly down at her small son, and the soft, iridescent glow of the star seemed to cast a gentle halo of light all around him. And it was gone, and she shook her head like one who wishes to make certain of her alertness.

When they got home, she was still troubled by it. She helped the boy undress, and she tucked him in with more care and tenderness than usual. When he asked her to help him with his prayers, she did—and she added a special, new prayer of her own. "Dear Father," she said, "I'm not sure just what happened tonight, but thank You."

When she returned to the living room, her husband, without looking up from the TV, said, "Well, how did it go?"

"If you really cared how it went, you might try going sometime. It went about the same as last year when you didn't go with us—except . . ." Her voice trailed off into silence, and she couldn't find a way of finishing.

He looked up from the show he was watching. "Except what? Did something happen?"

"No, nothing you would be interested in."

"Hey, I'm sorry I didn't go.

Did I miss something?"

"Yes, as a matter of fact, you *did* miss something. You missed being with your son and making him think he is more important than that stupid show. You missed being with me and letting me know that I am more important than that stupid show. You missed a lot of things, Andy, but tonight you missed something—something *really* special."

She paused, her heart beating wildly because she knew she was making a leap into the darkness, but she knew she had to take the chance. She picked up the remote control and turned the TV off.

"You're really cranked up about this, aren't you? Did something happen?"

"Yes," she said. "Yes, something *did* happen, Andy— at least I think it did, although I'm not sure just what— but it's not what happened that really matters. What matters is that it made me start thinking, and we need to talk."

And they did, you know.

They talked and talked.

And things were never the same again.

At some point in every holiday season, I find myself gazing at the stars. They seem especially close and significant when it's cold and silent. I think I want to see *that* star, at least to imagine the *wonder* of it, as it makes its majestic and purposeful way to its appointed destination. There, where it concentrates its glorious radiance on the holy ground, is where Jesus was born. God, calling to us,

"Look over here.

See My Incarnation."

It's not too hard for me to believe in *that* star. My childlike heart, awakened from months of slumber by this blessed season, is fully confident that the star's guiding light brought those wise men to worship Jesus. I wonder, though, where did it go? Does God still move stars to serve His purpose? Is there yet a light calling us to Bethlehem? Does His star not shine for us because we have grown so mature and practical that we dismiss it, as Scrooge dismissed his ghosts by uttering a "Humbug!" of disbelief?

The great man is he who does not lose his child's heart.

MENCIUS

The star was for *all* to see, but only the wise men were guided by it. When they arrived, they did not find multitudes of seekers who had also followed its light. Perhaps the guiding light of God's special star is there yet, but our eyes are not pointed upward to Him—because we do not believe in stars. Our eyes look inward to our own

wisdom and outward to our own light and around us to the light and wisdom of people like ourselves. And all the while, God calls us by His light, pleading with us to look upward to His holiness.

A child's imagination is a marvelous gift of God. Encourage it; strengthen it. The world will be struck real all too soon—you needn't worry about that. Sometimes we would all do well to see God through the eyes of a child. All together too many imaginations are ridiculed and discouraged by grownups who no longer have the capacity to dream.

Where did it go?

See that you
do not look down on
one of these little ones.
For I tell you that
their angels in heaven
always see the face
of my Father in heaven.

MATTHEW 18:10

Now faith is
being sure of
what we hope for
and certain of
what we do not see.

HEBREWS 11:1

He has not learned
the lesson of life
who does not
every day surmount
a fear.

RALPH WALDO EMERSON

THE OTHER SIDE OF FEAR

I was eight that summer—the summer of forty-five. So were James, Tommy, and Doug. It was another turning point in my life, although I didn't know anything about turning points and I certainly didn't mean for it to be.

I had much simpler things in mind.

The Great War ended that summer, and our brothers, husbands, uncles, fathers, and sons came home—at least many of them did. The dark cloud of war passed away, and great exuberance, hope, and lightheartedness seemed to settle over the country. Everybody was happy and carefree; people laughed more and sang more. The weather was great, the gardens were producing a bumper crop, the lyrics to popular music became brighter, people were getting married in droves, and even the sermons at church seemed to be less somber and threatening. School was out, and I had three months of nothing ahead of me but swimming, fishing, baseball, and roaming the countryside.

What a time to be alive.

The salt water swimming pool was right down the hill from our house. Looking back, it seems very strange that there should be a swimming pool near us, because we lived in a very sparsely settled, rural area. How it got there and why it was there still puzzles me, but it was there—right on the corner of Clark Road and Rochester Road.

It cost a quarter to get in. I never had one, but the people who owned it were very understanding and would let me do odd jobs for the price of admission. I started going there when I was five, I think. It had two diving boards, one about three feet off the water and one about twelve. The first year I went, I watched with envy and admiration as the older boys strode with measured, rhythmic steps to the end of the diving boards, jumped high, pushed down hard, and allowed the spring of the boards to propel them high into the air as they dove gracefully into the water. I walked out on the three-foot board in 1943, when I was six. I remember the growing fear, the queasiness in my stomach, as I gingerly edged my way to the end. When I looked down, the water was unbelievably far away. I closed my eyes and jumped—shocked at how soon I hit the water. Before the summer was over, I was jumping and diving regularly and fearlessly, and I began to look apprehensively at the twelve-foot board.

The next summer, when I was seven, my friends and I made a pact that we would conquer the twelve-foot board. I was the first to try it. I walked out slowly—careful to stay in the middle lest I fall off—and I looked down. The distance to the water was staggering. I stood long at the end of the board, my friends taunting me, but the dizzying nausea in my stomach made my legs weak and broke my will. I was absolutely frozen with fear, and gently, ever so slowly, I placed one foot behind the other and retreated to the safety of the platform. Several days passed, and all of my friends succeeded before I tried it again. Once again, by the end of summer, it was a regular thing.

There was another board.

It wasn't a diving board, really, and you are going to have to use your imagination to see this—and you really must see it to appreciate it. An iron pipe about four inches in diameter had been sunk into the concrete immediately in front of the platforms that supported the diving boards. It was attached, for stability, to the platforms at both levels, and it rose some ten or fifteen feet above the twelve-foot platform. Iron rungs, so small in diameter that they hurt your feet, had been welded to the pipe—beginning at the twelve-foot level. At the top of the iron pipe was a socket into which was placed a flagpole, and attached to the pipe, right at the socket, was a small platform about eight inches wide and two feet long. During the summer of forty-five, Tommy, Doug, James, and I vowed we would dive from that platform.

Faith is not belief without proof, but trust without reservation.
ELTON TRUEBLOOD

I went up the ladder twice, early that summer, to insert the flagpole into its place. Going up was relatively easy, because the tendency is to fix your eyes on your destination and you don't have to look down or feel for the rungs—

like you do on the way down.

Once the flag was in place, I would first look around, amazed at what I could see from my vantage point. Then my eyes would be drawn down—down to the water. That sick, nauseous feeling and the frightening dizziness would come, causing me to cling to the ladder desperately. I would close my eyes, establish my equilibrium, and very slowly begin searching for the next lowest rung and then the next, knowing that I must not open my eyes until I felt the wooden platform.

Tommy tried it first. It was July. He made it to the top of the ladder all right, but he had to be pried loose by the lifeguard, because he got so scared he wouldn't release his grip. His pleas for help caused all of us to be very sober. Two weeks later, Doug tried it; he did better. He made it to the top of the ladder, but the pipe ended at the flagpole socket, so you had to hold on to the flagpole itself as you climbed the last three rungs—and the flagpole wasn't very steady with the wind pulling the flag and bending the pole. Balancing was very tricky. Doug tried to crawl onto the platform on his hands and knees, but it was too small. In the process—
he lost his nerve and nearly fell.

August came and time grew short—the summer of forty-five was almost at an end. Doug moved away in the middle of August, and we never saw him again—it took some of the spirit out of our resolve. Every day I would stand and look up at the flagpole. The joy of the other boards was greatly diminished, and the pool wasn't as much fun as it had been. One morning it rained, but early in the afternoon, the sun came out for a short time. I went to the pool alone. I knew what I was going to do. I practiced climbing the ladder. I must have gone up and down twenty times or more. I was determined to conquer my fear of the ladder. Finally, I was able to rest at the top—and even look down—without getting sick and dizzy. I made a plan for how to get out on the board. I memorized every handhold and movement. I knew I must do it quickly—I must never hesitate, never consider what could go wrong—and once on the board, I must dive immediately.

That night I prayed much about it, and the next day I did it. I did it just like I had planned. I stepped out on the board, closed my eyes, and without hesitation—I dove.

It seemed an eternity before I hit the water.

Words will fail me here. It is truly amazing how many sensations can be experienced in so brief a moment—the acceleration as I sliced through the air on the way to the water, the incredible jolt as I hit the water, my hands slamming into the bottom of the pool almost immediately, bursting to the surface, swimming leisurely to the steps, being congratulated by my friends, and then standing there looking at the platform where I had just been. It was overwhelming—too much, too quickly. Fear, excitement, joy, satisfaction, relief, pride, exultation—they were all mine in a few seconds. I think I know how David felt when he walked out to face Goliath—when he saw that stone find its mark and Goliath drop to the ground dead. I knew what feelings must have gone through his mind as the entire Israelite army cheered and the Philistines ran.

It was amazing how different that platform looked *from the other side.*

Very few times in all my years have I experienced that type of complete satisfaction. I was on *the other side of fear,* the affirmative side—the side you can only know about if you have the faith to pass through fear. Those whose unbelief causes them to back away from fear on the front side only know fear as a deterrent—only experience the nausea, the dizziness, the paralyzing, terrifying frustration of defeat.

I have been afraid many times since the summer of forty-five. I have experienced all of its effects—down to the sweaty palms—but I believe that the summer of forty-five established a precedent for moving through fear. Just as fear increases if we respond negatively to it, so those who pass through—those who experience the other side of fear, the positive side—are those for whom fear becomes an incentive. They still experience the *symptoms* of fear, but those very symptoms become a source of motivation because they anticipate the other side.

The other side of fear—
no one can take you through it.
You must climb the ladder alone—
take the dive alone.
And you must do it by faith.

The LORD himself
goes before you and
will be with you;
he will never leave you
nor forsake you.
Do not be afraid;
do not be discouraged.

DEUTERONOMY 31:8

Courage is
resistance to fear,
mastery of fear,
not absence
of fear.

MARK TWAIN

When a man
heartily confesses,
leaving excuse to God,
the truth makes him free;
he knows that
the evil has gone from him,
as a man knows
that he is
cured of his plague.

GEORGE MACDONALD

GOD AND THE NICKEL

When I was a boy, pop was only a nickel. In other places they called it "Coke"—even if it wasn't—or "soda"—but we always called it "pop," and it was only a nickel. I know it's hard to believe, but unless you understand that, you won't get much out of this story. Nickels were hard to come by—that's why pop was a nickel—something about economics and the law of supply and demand. Anyway, there was this Standard Oil gas station on the corner of Eighteen Mile Road and Rochester Road, which was about a half mile from my house. It was owned by a guy named Marshall Bruder, which isn't too important, but it's neat to know if you're into that sort of thing.

Well, Marshall Bruder sold candy out of a glass case, and he had a red pop machine with

"Coca Cola" written in white cursive letters on the side. It was one of those old kinds of machines that had ice and real cold water in the bottom, and the bottles of pop sat right down in the water. That's what made them cold, in case you're a little slow on the uptake, and that's also what made them so desirable—the pop, I mean. You don't ever see ads saying,

"Get your room-temperature pop right here."

On real hot days in the summertime, I used to go to Marshall Bruder's with Tommy and Freddy Peterson. We used to go to Marshall Bruder's Standard Oil gas station because the concrete floors inside were smooth and cool on our bare feet and because we would open the lid of the pop machine and stick our hands way down deep—up to our elbows—in that ice-cold water. It was delicious. Mrs. Bruder would eventually run us out. Not too quickly, though—and she wasn't mean or anything. When we left, we'd get a drink out of their artesian well. The water was cold and sweet. They had this rock wall all around the well, and it formed a sort of pool—very small, but it was a neat place to play.

I want to get back to the pop machine, though. Every time I opened that lid, I would think about

> *Our prayer and God's mercy are like two buckets in a well; while one ascends, the other descends.*
>
> ARTHUR HOPKINS

how neat it would be to say, "Gimme a pop"—just like my dad or other grown-ups who came into Marshall Bruder's. "Gimme a pop." I used to practice saying it when I was alone. I'd walk down Clark Road saying, "Gimme a pop." I'd walk around the house saying, "Gimme a pop." My mother would say, "What did you say?" and I'd say, "Oh, nothin'." They had Coca Cola, but they also had R.C. Cola, Byerly's Grape, and Nesbitt's Orange. That was what I really wanted. I had it all figured out. When Mr. Bruder would say, "What kind of pop?" I'd say, "Nesbitt's Orange." But I never had a nickel—neither did Tommy or Freddy. Things grow in a child's mind—they get out of proportion, and that's what led me to do something unthinkable.

We went to a small church that met in a Masonic lodge in Hazel Park, Michigan. My dad led singing; another guy—Bob Winegar—did too, but my dad was the *real* song leader. Brother Utley was the preacher. It was a real good church. I liked going to church there because Brother Utley was a soft-spoken, kindly sort of man who talked to the kids like they were people, and he got the boys up in front and asked us Bible questions and taught us to lead singing, and he never yelled or scared me. When my dad led singing, he made me want to sing because he so obviously enjoyed himself.

After communion they took up the collection. It was sort of confusing to me, because when they took up the collection, they always said it was "separate and apart" from the Lord's Supper—but even a child could see that it wasn't.

The money went in these wicker baskets with green velvet bottoms. The bottoms were soft like that, so you wouldn't be embarrassed when you dropped change in the basket. I figured that out by myself. When it was all collected, they put the baskets with the money up front under the communion table. I don't know if the idea seized me all at once or if it crept over me very subtly and slowly. I only know that one Sunday after church—while everybody was outside visiting because it was so hot inside—I went back inside, walked right up to the communion table, and took a nickel out of the collection plate. I guess I thought that God wouldn't mind losing a lousy nickel for a bottle of pop—I mean, what's a nickel to God? It's very important that you understand that I could have taken anything—a five-dollar bill, even. But I didn't want a five-dollar bill.

I wanted a nickel—wanted one so badly

that I risked going to hell to get it.

Nobody ever knew. I put it in my pocket, and the next day when Tommy, Freddy, and I went to Marshall Bruder's, I had it with me. But when the time came to say, "Gimme a pop," I couldn't do it—I mean, the words just wouldn't come out, and it scared me because I would try to say the words, and I couldn't. I tried it again the next day, and it was worse, so I put the nickel in a shoe under my bed, and I didn't touch it again. But it haunted me. I couldn't get that nickel out of my mind. I couldn't sleep, and when I did I had terrible dreams. God would speak to me. He would say in a very loud voice,

"Where is My nickel? I want My nickel."

God was so *real* to me—so incredibly, practically *real*, and I realized I had done a terrible thing—committed a sin beyond reckoning. I had stolen money right out of God's very own pocket—

and I was terrified.

I couldn't wait for the next Sunday to come. I was so anxious to get to church that I was in a sweat. I prayed that God would just let me live long enough to put that nickel in the collection tray when it was passed, so the nightmare would be over and I would know that I was forgiven.

Sunday came. When we got to church, I couldn't sing—somehow it didn't seem right—and I didn't hear anything Brother Utley said. All I could think about was that nickel in my pocket—and *here I was, right in God's very presence,* and anything could happen. Brother Utley might stop any moment and say, "We have a thief in our midst," and every eye would turn toward me, because somehow they would know. They might prove who stole it by casting lots—like they did with Achan—and I knew that I would get the short stick and they would stone me to death.

My mother had given me a coin to put in the collection tray, but as it came, I found it impossible to put the extra nickel in without detection, because we sat up front and there wasn't anything else in the basket.

My plan was foiled.

After church everybody went outside just like the week before. I crept very carefully back in, but this time with *much fear and reverence*. Like a Jew approaching the ark of the covenant, I approached the communion table. I was trembling from head to foot—absolutely terror stricken. I bent over and prayed a little prayer: "God, please forgive me for stealing this nickel. I promise I'll never do it again. In Jesus's name, amen." I placed the nickel, very gently, back into the collection tray and ran out of the building as rapidly as I could.

I was so happy, so relieved, so forgiven. No prisoner ever experienced a greater thrill of freedom and forgiveness. God had graciously made it possible for me to come back into His presence. I felt so good that I sang church songs in the backseat of the car on the way home.

I acknowledged
my sin to you and did not
cover up my iniquity.
I said, "I will confess
my transgressions
to the LORD"~
and you forgave
the guilt of my sin.

PSALM 32:5

What we obtain
too cheap,
we esteem too lightly;
it is dearness
only that gives
everything its value.

Thomas Paine

VALUE

On Clark Road we had a grape arbor. Huge clusters of dark, purple, Concord grapes grew there. I was nuts about them (maybe I should say *grapes* about them). As soon as they were ripe—and sometimes before—I would pull a whole cluster and pinch the thin skins between my thumb and forefinger, squeezing the purple juice and greenish pulpy mass inside my mouth. I got so good at it that I could do a grape about every two seconds. But no matter how hard I tried, I couldn't even make a dent in the overall population of grapes. I would leave huge piles of skins where I had stood—

but the vines looked
untouched.

Before the first frost,
my mom and I would make
grape juice. We'd gather

bushels of grapes—pull them from the stems, wash them, sort them, getting out the unripe and the rotten—and then we'd put them in cheesecloth and crush them, collecting the beautiful, dark, clear juice in a huge pan. My memory fails me on some parts of the process from that point. I know we dipped the Ball jars—which we had saved from last year—in boiling water. Then we poured in the juice, poured a layer of paraffin wax on top, put on a seal, and screwed on the lid. My dad always did that part because he could get it tighter that anyone else. We made quite a bit, and it was very good. We kept it in the fruit cellar under the house.

During the winter and into the spring, we would open a jar occasionally. My mother was very frugal by nature, and she rationed the grape juice out to us in what seemed thimblefuls— every mouthful was treasured. There was no swilling it down in huge gulps; a small glass was sipped carefully, lasting all evening.

Grape juice was *valuable* stuff.

I suppose it wasn't particularly good grape juice by today's standards. We didn't strain it as well as we would have liked, so there was a lot of sediment at the bottom. I could never get the paraffin sealer out cleanly, so pieces of wax were always floating in it. My mother put very little sugar in it—we couldn't afford that—so some of it was quite bitter. Invariably, toward spring, some of it would begin to ferment, due to a hole in the paraffin or a lid not sealed properly—

but we drank it anyway.

It was the highlight of every holiday, birthday, or occasion, and I felt like royalty every time I was sent to the cellar to get a jar. It seemed an eternity between the last of it and the new crop.

What made me think about making grape juice is that I just returned from the refrigerator. Inside is a half-gallon plastic container filled with Welch's—well, it *was* filled; it's about half-empty now. This grape juice comes frozen in a can, it has no sediment, it is absolutely uniform in taste, there are never pieces of paraffin in it, and it never ferments. There is no picking, sorting, crushing, or boiling—you just add water. I just drained a sixteen-ounce glass in two draughts. I hardly noticed the taste. It cost me almost nothing. I do not fear running out. Our freezer has several cans.

I pay no attention.

It's an old story, a lesson told and retold by succeeding generations of parents and teachers from the beginning of time. Its truth is ageless and bottomless. I never learn it so completely that the next time it washes over me I do not feel it fresh—the lesson of *value*. What makes things have worth?

It is always what I pay—
what it cost—
how much suffering
or love goes into it!
A thing's value is in direct proportion to how much of myself I have invested in it.

The only thing
that makes one place
more attractive
to me than another
is the quantity of heart
I find in it.

Jane Welsh Carlyle

Believe in the sun,
even when
it does not shine.
Believe in love,
even when
you do not feel it.
Believe in God,
even when
you do not see Him.

Hans Kung

A CHRISTMAS MEMORY

In 1946 we had Christmas dinner at Aunt Velma's. I was nine. Aunt Velma was my mother's youngest sister. She was married to my uncle Brett Snoddy—pronounced, *Snow'-dee*. They were always pretty touchy about their last name, so I want to make sure I don't offend them— though I haven't seen any of them for thirty years, at least.

Aunt Velma had five children: Brett Jr., Bobby, Sidney, Nancy, and David. David was my age, and Nancy was my sister's age. Brett Jr. and Bobby were much older than I.

In 1946 the Snoddys were living in a log house— it had an open ceiling with big log support beams. It was a fascinating place. Anyway, Brett Jr. and

Bobby had been drafted, because of the war, and I had not seen them in a long time. But now the war was over, and they were going to be home for Christmas.

We got there pretty early, and we opened presents. Brett Jr. was there when we got there, but Bobby wasn't, and I could tell that Aunt Velma was upset about it. I heard her tell my mom that Bobby had called and said he was trying to hitchhike because he didn't have money for a bus.

The day went by pretty quickly for me. We built a huge and elaborate snowman, complete with a carrot nose, charcoal eyes and ears, and a top hat and scarf. Then we had a snowball fight, after which we went ice-skating on the creek that ran near their house. By dinnertime I was famished Aunt Velma postponed dinner as long as she could—but Bobby didn't show. Finally, we sat down to eat without him. Aunt Velma set a place for Bobby, and she put a chair for him at the table. I think it sort of made everybody solemn—

looking at that empty chair.

The Snoddys weren't religious people, and usually they just dove right into whatever was on the table, but today Aunt Velma asked my dad to pray that God would take care of her Bobby and send him home. Her voice was all shaky and choked up, and when I looked at her, I saw that she was crying—the tears were running down her cheeks and

dripping right onto her plate.

Everybody got real sad. We all bowed our heads, but for some reason, my dad didn't get right into his prayer, and when he did, it was a lot different from the one he usually prayed—the one I could say by heart. When he finished, it was pretty quiet for a while, but then we started passing things and eating and talking, and everybody sort of got loosened up—like you always do—and we laughed and told stories. Even Aunt Velma joined in. It was a great dinner.

We were eating dessert when it happened—I mean, we had totally forgotten—

but He hadn't.

One of the boys said, "Somebody just pulled into the driveway," and everything stopped, but nobody moved. Then a car door slammed, and there was a knock on the door. It's funny how you react to things. Everybody just sat and looked at each other—everybody but Aunt Velma. She was already up serving dessert.

"It's Bobby," she cried. "God has sent Bobby home; I just know He has."

"Now Velma, don't get your hopes up," Uncle Brett said. "It's probably someone else."

Everybody started to get up, but nobody could beat Aunt Velma to the door. She was determined that it was Bobby—

and it was.

I don't know what anybody else thought, because we didn't talk about it, but I never doubted for one minute that God had sent Bobby home—

and I still don't doubt it.

You believe
that easily
which you hope
for earnestly.

Terence

The kingdom of heaven
is like a merchant
looking for fine pearls.
When he found one
of great value,
he went away and
sold everything he had,
and bought it.

MATTHEW 13:45 – 46

THE PERFECT PERI

Marbles was the game we played. There was no basket or ball for basketball, no one owned a football, baseball took too much time for recess or lunch hour—so we played marbles. We drew circles about five feet in diameter in the dirt, and everyone contributed a pre-arranged number of marbles to go inside the circle, which we called "the pot." We played for keeps. If you hit a marble with your shooter and knocked it outside the line that marked the pot, it was yours. There were rules against hunching, eyedroppers, and throwing.

There were three basic kinds of marbles—aggies, steelies, and peries. Everybody had a favorite shooter, a special marble prized above all the others. Mine was a perfect peri. I do not know the derivation of that word, and I spelled it by ear. I only know that we used it to signify a marble that was above average in size, perfectly clear, and perfectly round. There were only two or three in the entire school, so a peri was considered quite a prize.

My teacher, Miss Smokey, allowed marbles on the playground, marbles in the pockets, and marbles in your desk; but any marble in her classroom that became *visible*—was hers. She collected hundreds during the course of the year. A boy, who had suffered some severe losses to my peri and who was extremely envious, persuaded me to show it to him in the boys' bathroom. When I produced it, he slapped it out of my hand and ran to Miss Smokey. She took it. I mourned the loss of my shooter like a lost friend.

Since Miss Smokey had no use for marbles, she had devised a fascinating way of giving them back. Late in the spring, she would take her hoard of marbles and place it on top of her desk. She had the boys line up behind the desk (girls did not play marbles in our school), and then she would tip over the box, and we would scramble after them.

I lined up in a very advantageous position, having remembered where

Everything is worth what its purchaser will pay for it.
PUBLILIUS SYRUS

most of the marbles went the previous year, and consequently seized upward of a hundred marbles—

but not the one I wanted.

It was found by a third grader. I offered him a penny for it, but he declined. I offered to bust his head if he didn't give it to me, but he declined that offer also—and since he had an eighth-grade brother, I didn't push the issue. I was determined to get my shooter, and I finally asked what he would take for it. He said that he would trade me the peri for the hundred marbles I had captured.

It wasn't hard.

I mean, I never hesitated. He could have asked for every marble I owned, and I would have gladly given them to him. I was so glad to get my shooter back that I thought I had made the best deal of my life. All those other marbles meant nothing to me. I carried my shooter home, stopping along the way to take it out of my pocket and hold it up to the sunlight to admire its flawless perfection—

and I was happy.

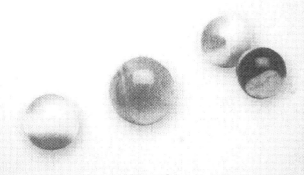

Value is the
life~giving power
of anything;
cost, the quantity of labor
required to produce it;
price, the quantity of labor
which its possessor
will take
in exchange for it.

JOHN RUSKIN

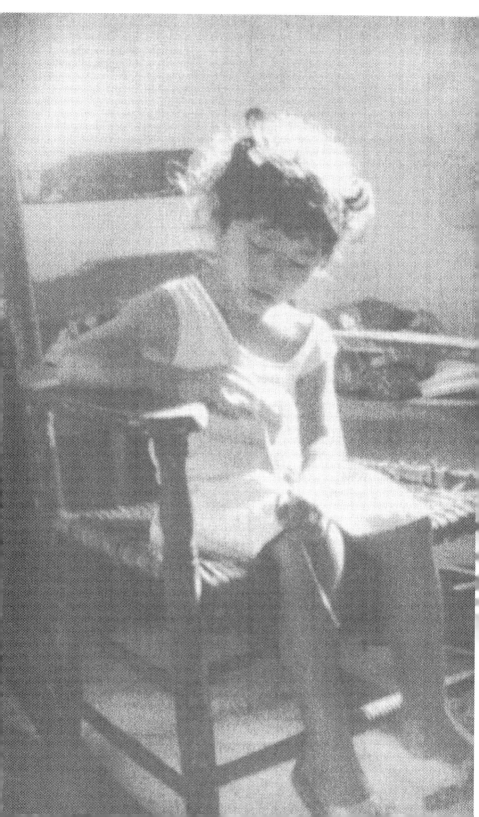

PART THREE

Lifelong Lessons

We need someone
to believe in us. . . .
The individual who thinks
well of you, who keeps his
mind on your good qualities,
and does not look
for flaws, is your friend.
Who is my brother?
I'll tell you: he is one who
recognizes the good in me.

ELBERT HUBBARD

THE WINNER

I was watching some little kids play soccer. I don't have little ones anymore, so I just watch them—and their parents. These kids were about five or six, I think. They were playing a real game—a serious game—two teams, complete with coaches, uniforms, and parents. I didn't know any of them, so I was able to enjoy the games without distraction of being anxious about winning or losing.

I wish the parents and coaches
could have done the same.

The teams were pretty evenly matched. I will just call them Team One and Team Two. The first period passed with nobody scoring. The kids were hilarious. They were clumsy and terribly inefficient. They fell over their own feet, they stumbled over the ball, they kicked at the ball and missed it—but they didn't seem to care.

It was fun.

In the second period, the Team One coach pulled out what must have been his first team

and put in the "scrubs"—except for his best player, who now guarded the goal. The game took a dramatic turn. I guess winning is important—even when you're five years old—because the Team Two coach left his best players in, and the Team One scrubs were no match for them. They swarmed about the little guy who was no match for three or four boys who were also very good. Team Two began to score.

The Team One goalie gave it everything he had, recklessly throwing his body in front of incoming balls, trying to stop them.

Team Two scored two goals in quick succession.

It infuriated the young boy. He became a raging maniac—shouting, running, diving. With all the stamina he could muster, he covered the boy who now had the ball, but that boy kicked it to another boy twenty feet away, and by the time he repositioned himself, it was too late.

They scored a third goal.

I soon learned who his parents were. They were nice, decent-looking people. I could tell that his dad had just come from the office—he was still wearing his suit and tie. They yelled encouragement to their son. I became totally absorbed in watching the boy on the field and his parents on the sidelines.

After the third goal, the little kid changed. He could see it was no use. He couldn't stop them, and he became frustrated. He didn't quit, but he became quietly desperate—

futility was written all over him.

His father changed too. He had been urging his son to try harder—yelling advice and encouragement. But then he changed. He became anxious. He tried to say that it was OK if they scored; he encouraged him to hang in there; he grieved for the pain in his son.

After the fourth goal, I knew what was going to happen. I have seen it before. *The boy needed help so badly, and there was none.* He retrieved the ball from the net and handed it to the referee—and then he cried.

He just stood there, while huge tears rolled down both cheeks. He went to his knees. He hated crying, but what else can you do when you're all alone and there's no help? He put his fists to his eyes—his grief and frustration were so great—and he cried the tears of the helpless and brokenhearted.

When the boy went to his knees, I saw the father start onto the field. His wife clutched his arm and said, "Jim, don't. You'll embarrass him." But he tore loose from her and ran right out onto the field. He wasn't supposed to—the game was still in progress. Suit, tie, dress shoes, and all—he charged onto the field. He picked up his son—so everybody would know he was his boy—and he hugged him and held him and cried with him.

I've never been so proud
of a man in my life.

He carried him off the field, and when he got close to the sidelines, I heard him say, "Scotty, I'm so proud of you. You were great out there. I wanted everybody to know that you were my son."

"Daddy," the boy sobbed, "I couldn't stop them. I did everything you told me. I

> *A life spent in making mistakes is not only more honorable but more useful than a life spent doing nothing.*
>
> GEORGE BERNARD SHAW

tried, Daddy, I tried and tried, and they scored on me."

"Scotty, it doesn't matter how many times they score on you. You're my son, and I'm proud of you. I want you to go back and play right now. *You can't stay out of the game, and you're going to get scored on again, but it doesn't matter to us.* Go on, now."

It made a difference—I could tell it did. When you're all alone and you're getting scored on and you can't stop them, it means a lot to know that it doesn't matter to those who love you. The little guy ran back on to the field. They scored two more times—

but it was OK.

Remember, parents—you *can't* keep your kids from getting scored on, you *can't* stop the pain, and you *can't* keep your children out of the game. You *can* let them know that you love them, that they don't have to win to get your approval, that you're proud of them in spite of the mistakes they make, and that you get "scored on" too. It makes a difference.

I get scored on every day. I try so hard. I throw my body recklessly in every direction. I fume and rage. The tears come, and I go to my knees—helpless and alone. And my Father—my heavenly Father, the God of the universe—rushes right out on the field—right in front of the whole crowd, the whole jeering, laughing world—and He picks me up and hugs me and says, "John, I'm so proud of you. You were great out there. I wanted everybody to know that you were My son, and because I control the outcome of this game, I declare you—

the Winner."

Every child will look
in the eyes of the Father,
and the eyes
of the Father will
receive the child with an
infinite embrace.

GEORGE MACDONALD

As a mother
comforts her child,
so will I
comfort you.

ISAIAH 66:13

Father, let me
hold Thy hand and
like a child walk
with Thee
down all my days,
secure in Thy love
and strength.

THOMAS Á KEMPIS

Run, Tami, Run

It was a marvelously bright, clear, cool morning, and hundreds of spectators had gathered on the hillsides to witness the Texas Regional Cross-Country Races at Mae Simmons Park. Most of the spectators were parents and family members who had traveled many miles—in some cases, hundreds—to watch just one race. Their faces were intent, their eyes always fastened on the only runner they were interested in; and often when the runners were far away and could not hear their shouts of encouragement, still their lips would move, mouthing the precious, familiar names—and *one other word.* Sometimes they would say the name audibly but softly, as if for no ears but their own, and yet it seemed that they hoped to be heard.

"*Run,* Jimmy," they whispered urgently.

"*Run,* Tracy.

Run."

The cross-country race is two miles for girls, three for boys. It is a grueling run—physically and mentally exhausting—over hills and rough terrain. There were ten races that morning, beginning with class 5A boys and girls. Each race had from eighty to one-hundred-twenty competitors. The course ended where it began, but at times the runners were nearly a half-mile away.

As the class 5A girls' race came to a close, I watched a forty-plus-year-old mother—who was wearing patent leather shoes and a skirt and carrying a purse—run the last hundred yards beside her daughter.

She saw no other runners. As she ran awkwardly, her long, dark hair came undone and was streaming out behind her. Giving no thought to the spectacle she made, she cried, "*Run,* Tami, *run! Run,* Tami, *run!*" There were hundreds of people crowing in, shouting and screaming, but this mother was determined to be heard. "*Run,* Tami, *run!*" she pleaded. The girl had no chance to win, and the voice of her mother, whose heart was bursting with exertion and emotion, was not urging her to win.

She was urging her to finish.

The girl was in trouble. Her muscles were cramping; her breath came in ragged gasps; her stride was broken. She was in the last stages of weariness, just before collapse. But when she heard her mother's voice, a marvelous transformation took place. The girl straightened, she found her balance, her bearing, her rhythm—and she *finished*. She crossed the finish line, turned, and collapsed into the arms of her mother.

They fell down together on the grass and they cried, and then they laughed. They were having the best time together, like there was no one else in the world but them. *God*, I thought, *this is beautiful. Thank You for letting me see it.*

As I drove away from Mae Simmons Park, I couldn't get that scene off my mind. A whole morning of outstanding performances had merged into a single happening. I thought of my own children and of a race they are running—a different and far more important race, a race that requires even greater stamina, courage, and character. I am a spectator in that race also. I have helped them train, I have pleaded, instructed, threatened, punished, prayed, praised, laughed, and cried. I have even tried to familiarize them with the course. But now the gun is up, and their race has begun, and I am a *spectator*. My heart is bursting—

I see no other runners.

Sometimes their course takes them far from me, and yet I whisper, "*Run*, children, *run*." They do not hear, but there is One who does. Occasionally, they grow weary because the race is long and demands such sacrifice. They witness hypocrisy, and there are many voices that call to them to quit this race, telling them that they cannot possibly win. They lose sight of their goal, and they falter and stumble—and I cry,

"*Run*, children, *run*. Please *run*."

And then they come to the last hundred yards—how I long to be there, to run beside them. What if I am gone, and there is no one to whisper, to shout, "*Run*" in their ears? What if they lose sight of the great truth that in this race, it is *finishing* that counts?

Dear God, please hear my prayer. If they cannot hear my voice, if I must watch from beyond this arena, please run beside them as You have so often run beside me. Strengthen their knees that they might finish. And when they cross that eternal finish line, may I be there to embrace them and welcome them home. May we cry and laugh and spend eternity together.

Remember though
thy foes are
strong and tried,
the angels of Heaven
are on thy side,
and God is over all!

ADELAIDE ANNE PROCTOR

I have loved you,
my people,
with an everlasting love.
With unfailing love
I have drawn you
to myself.

JEREMIAH 31:3

To overcome
difficulties is
to experience the
full delight
of existence.

ARTHUR SCHOPENHAUER

THE PINSON MOUNDS

I t was Friday night. I had been to Jackson, Tennessee, with my date and was now returning to the college we attended in Henderson. As we approached the thriving metropolis of Pinson—a city of seventy-five souls, known worldwide for the Pinson Mounds (nothing to do with candy bars)—the car started pulling radically to the left, which could only mean one thing: a flat tire. I swerved quickly into a roadside pull-out sheltered by oak trees.

Now the pullout wasn't such a bad place, especially in view of who I was with—and I was never one to cast aside lightly what had obviously been made available to me. But I knew I was going to have to do something eventually. Joan was very understanding, but she had to be back in the

dormitory by 10:30, or we would both have to stand trial before the D.C.—the Discipline Committee—to explain our whereabouts on the night in question. I had already had the dubious honor, if not pleasure, of receiving a personal invitation to appear before this venerated and august group of sages on several previous occasions and had no desire for a return engagement.

Across the street from the pullout was a one-stall, combination repair shop, junk dealer, post office, hardware store, gas station, *you-name-it-we-got-it* place. It had closed before dark, but the proprietor's house was next-door. It was my only hope. There were no lights on, and it was obvious that they were in bed. I knocked timidly at first, but getting no response and being rather desperate, I banged loudly. This aroused the dog who, from the sound he made, must have resembled King Kong. But fortunately, he was chained.

I began to hear the angry mutterings and rumblings of someone who obviously had a deep resentment toward this unwarranted disruption of his nocturnal bliss. A light went on, the door opened slightly, and then he appeared. His hair was disheveled, his pants, hastily thrown on over long underwear—which also served as his nighttime attire— hung by one suspender. He was barefoot, his eyes were half-open, and when he opened the door, he had a most unpleasant expression on his face.

"Good evening, sir," I said in my most cheerful, polite, and deferential tone.

"Good *morning*, you mean," he said— neither cheerfully, polite, nor deferentially. "It's got to be after midnight. Whadayawant?"

"I'm very sorry to inconvenience you, sir, but you see, I have a problem."

"Don't give me that *inconvenience* rubbish. Everybody's got problems, sonny—even me," he said as he looked sourly and suspiciously at me.

"Oh, really?" I said. "I'm sorry to hear that, but you see, I have a flat tire."

"Come back tomorrow." He started to close the door.

"But I can't do that." Desperation was edging into my voice. "I'm from Freed-Hardeman, over in Henderson, and my girl has to be in the dorm by 10:30, and if I don't get her there, we'll be in big trouble." I tried to slide my foot forward so he couldn't close the door.

"Put your spare tire on."

"Well, sir, that's another problem. I don't *exactly* have a spare tire."

He emitted a long sigh of resignation and hopelessness—the kind of sigh that every parent learns all too quickly.

"Where's your car, Sonny?"

"Right over there behind those oaks," I said, as I pointed across the road.

"OK. You go get the tire off and bring it over, and I'll fix it."

"Yes, sir," I said enthusiastically, "But—well—actually, you see, I don't *exactly* have a jack either."

"Don't *exactly* have a jack? Son, either you have a jack or you don't have a jack.

What *exactly* do you have? Do you have one *approximately*? Oh, forget it. There's one in that shed there beside the shop. Don't let Old Walt scare you; he's chained up. He sounds real fierce, but he's never *exactly* hurt anybody—seriously."

"Say, thanks a lot. You—uh—you wouldn't happen to have a lug wrench, would you?"

"Oh, please, why me?" he muttered under his breath. "Yeah, there should be one in there with the jack," he said aloud. "Anything else you don't *exactly* have?"

"No, sir," I said confidently. "That ought to just about do it."

It turned out that the jack was just about a foot from the end of Old Walt's chain, which looked very fragile. Old Walt was a bit much. He looked like a cross between a grizzly bear and a mountain lion, and he acted as if he hadn't eaten in six weeks. He absolutely terrified me—lunging so hard against the end of his chain that he actually dragged his house, to which the chain was attached, behind him. His snarl began somewhere in the pit of his stomach, and by the time it came ripping, hissing, rattling, and roaring out his throat, it sounded like an avalanche. His eyes looked like laser beams, he had foam around his mouth, saliva dripped from his jaws, and when he snapped and ground his huge teeth, sparks flew. Old Walt was the original and archetypal *junkyard dog.* I found a piece of rope, lassoed the jack, and dragged it close enough to me that I could grab it and run.

As I took the lug nuts off, I placed them in the hubcap for safekeeping. It was totally dark where the car was, and I had been too ashamed to ask for a flashlight, which I didn't *exactly* have either. The rim was rusted tightly to the drum, and I had to kick it with all my might to break it loose. When it finally flew off, it hit the edge of the hubcap and scattered the lug nuts in every direction, mostly under the car. I could only find one because the ground was about three inches deep in oak leaves. To make matters worse, I also discovered that I could *see through* my tire. It was absolutely ruined, and so was the inner tube. When I crossed the road again, tire in hand, I was simply wretched. My benefactor was in the garage.

"I don't think this tire is any good," I said apologetically. "You don't *happen* to have one, do you?"

"I don't *happen* to have nothin', sonny. What I got here, I got on *purpose*, and I do have one." He rummaged around and eventually found a pretty decent tire.

"I could let you have this one for five bucks."

"Do you have one any less expensive? I don't *exactly* have five dollars," I said.

"How *much* less expensive? Maybe I could let it go for three," he said.

"I don't *exactly* have three either."

"Well, how much *exactly* do you have?" he said with exasperation.

"Well, if you put it in *exact* terms." I reached in my front pocket and counted out the change. "I

have thirty-five cents," I said hopefully.

At that very moment, Joan appeared. She had grown tired of waiting and had come to see if I was making any progress.

Joan was very, very pretty.

"Who in the world is this?" he said, with a whistle and obvious admiration in his voice.

"Oh, this is Joan; she's my date."

He looked appreciatively at Joan.

"You sure must be some *talker*, sonny. She sure didn't go with you for your looks, your money, your brains, or your car."

A pretty girl does wonders to men. In the presence of Joan, his whole attitude changed. He became gracious, kind, even cheerful—he forgot his inconvenience. He *gave* me the tire, found a tube, patched it, found some spare lug nuts, and helped me put it on. He even invited me to stop by and visit him on my next trip to Jackson—

if I brought Joan.

He smiled when I told him I would try to repay him someday. "Oh," he said, "that's OK. Forget it. I'll get more than my money's worth telling this story over the next twenty-five years. But nobody will believe it."

It wasn't until I got back to my room that I began to realize that I had just learned something about grace. I had learned what it means to be totally helpless, to have absolutely nothing in your hands but your need, and to receive a gift that is offered to you cheerfully and at personal cost—

a gift you can never repay.

What wisdom
can you find that
is greater
than kindness?

JEAN JACQUES ROUSSEAU

Prayer is the wing
wherewith the soul
flies to heaven,
and meditation the eye
wherewith we see God.

SAINT AMBROSE

In the all~important world
of family relations,
three words are
almost as powerful
as the famous,
"I love you."
They are
"Maybe you're right."

 OREN ARNOLD

GERTRUDE

My son Lincoln and I had been to the town of Frankenmuth, Michigan, to fish. He was about eleven at the time. The town is only about fifty miles from Flint, where we lived, and is nearly world famous for its breweries and for Zenders— a national monument to fried chicken and sauerbraten. It is much less well known for salmon fishing, but that's why we went there. The Clinton River is dammed there, and the Lake Huron salmon collect below the dam.

We drove over right after school, hoping to fish a couple of hours before dark. It was late fall. When we headed home after a very successful trip, it was cold and very dark. We were speeding along a narrow, twisting country road, when suddenly my headlights revealed a white duck in the middle of the road. I can't imagine what it was doing in the road at that time of night. I thought ducks were like chickens and went to sleep as soon as it got dark—and this one should have. I was going much too fast to swerve, and there was no time to stop. I heard the sickening *whack* and *crunch* of the duck hitting the underside of the car repeatedly.

It isn't easy to explain my next action—in fact, it's a little embarrassing—but I have to try, or I can't tell the rest of the story. You need to know me personally, and you need to understand the way I was brought up. In my family, nothing was ever wasted.

It was a sin to waste.

I turned around and went back to pick up the duck so we could take it home and eat it. It was lying in a heap, sprawled out in obvious death in the middle of ten thousand feathers. I pulled up alongside, reached out my door, picked up the duck, laid it on the floor behind my seat, and headed home once again.

Lincoln was very quiet as we drove, but completely alert. Normally, he would have been sound asleep after such a day, but the incident with the duck had totally captured his imagination. I noticed that he kept looking behind my seat. A few minutes later, he said,

"Dad, do ducks have souls?"

"No, Son, ducks don't have souls."

"What happens to a duck when it dies?"

"We eat it."

"I mean, where does it go?"

"It doesn't go anywhere. It just *isn't* anymore."

"Oh." He thought for a few minutes and then he said, "Dad, is it OK to pray for a duck?"

"I guess so, but why would you want to?"

"I feel sorry for it."

He lapsed into a thoughtful silence, and I assumed that he was praying. He kept his eyes on the duck, and a few minutes later, he spoke again.

"Dad?"

"What, Son?"

"God just answered my prayer; that duck's alive."

"Son, that duck is dead."

A few minutes passed.

"Dad, the duck is alive. I just saw it move."

"No, Son, the duck may have moved from the motion of the car, but that duck is not alive. I know you feel sorry for the duck, and I do too. And I know you prayed for the duck, but we have to learn to accept bad things in life. *The duck is dead.* You heard it hit the car, didn't you?"

"Yes, but Dad, the duck just moved again, and it's not the motion of the car. *It's looking right at me.*"

"Son, this has gone far enough. You mustn't allow your imagination to run away with you. I've told you that the duck is dead. *It is dead!* No amount of wishful thinking can bring it back. Trust me. I'm your father, and when I tell you that the duck is dead, you can believe me.

The duck is dead!

Now, I don't want to hear any more about that duck.

Do you understand?"

"Yes, sir."

"*Quack.*"

"What was that noise?"

"I think it was the dead duck, Dad."

I turned around, and sure enough, there was the duck, standing up and looking rather puzzled by its new surroundings.

"Son," I said, "it must be a miracle, because that duck was dead!"

We took it home, fed it, found a marvelous place for it to stay—in our swimming pool, which was closed for the winter anyway—and we named her (I guess it was a her) Gertrude. About a month later we went back to Frankenmuth. We took Gertrude and released her as near to the spot where we had found her as possible and went on our way.

I learned a lesson from Gertrude the duck that day. I learned that I'm not always right. I learned that older isn't always wiser, I learned that sometimes we allow our presuppositions to override obvious facts, and I learned that if I insist on being right and won't even listen to another point of view, I might be forced to acknowledge my fallibility by a loud "quack" of reality.

The next time you feel compelled to stand your ground, no matter the facts, just remember Gertrude the duck and relax a little. Learn the grace of laughing at yourself. It really isn't so bad to admit that you're wrong—

once in a while.

He who trusts
in himself is a fool,
but he who walks
in wisdom
is kept safe.

PROVERBS 28:26

God has his
small interpreters,
the child must
teach the man.

JOHN GREENLEAF WHITTIER

The Lord of gladness
delights in
the laughter
of a merry heart.

GEORGE MACDONALD

Saturday Morning

Saturday mornings are special. They're meant for late, great breakfasts—for walking around the neighborhood, getting and contributing to the local gossip—for running unimportant errands and for just being lazy in general. They seldom work out that way, but that's what they're for.

The schedule for this particular Saturday was all fouled up, but I was determined to get it *unfouled*, so I worked it all out. I would get up at 7:00, leave at 7:40, get to the post office when it opened at 8:00, mail my packages, leave at 8:15, arrive at the appliance dealer at 8:30, get the part I needed for the washing machine, and be home by 9:00. I should finish the repair job by 9:30 and have the rest of my Saturday to wile away in the appropriate fashion I have described above.

It all started wonderfully. I got up—and I *almost* left on time. I bounced energetically up to the post office steps whistling "Yankee Doodle," and I came face to face with a sign that read, *Closed on Saturdays*. My shock and chagrin were indescribable. The good, old, ever-lovin', dependable—rain, shine, sleet, and snow—post office was not open!

I was frosted.

Just shows what shape this country is in. Back in 1947, when I worked for the post office, back in *the good old days* when men were men and women were . . . sweet potatoes—well, something different than what they are now—anyway, back then, the post office opened at 8:00 sharp, every day—except, of course, Sundays; and we knew that nothing ought to be open on Sundays, except, of course, churches and Big Daddy's Delightful Diner.

I shuffled back to my car, muttering under my breath words too wonderful for language— my schedule shot, my whole morning thrown out of rhythm. I bought a copy of the local paper, the *Avalanche Journal*, to pass the time before the appliance store opened. Now you must understand that I lived in Lubbock, Texas, where the nearest thing to a hill is the overpass on the interstate highway. I read that title again—*Avalanche*

Journal—how could anybody in Lubbock, Texas, know anything about avalanches? You've got to have mountains for avalanches; this place doesn't even have a hill. Nobody around here has ever seen anything slide, much less an avalanche—there's no place to slide *down*, no place to slide *to. Avalanche Journal*—the guy who named this paper must have been a blind poet who moved here from Colorado

after he went blind.

Finally, the appliance store opened. I ran in and got my part and drove home. But the time I arrived, I was in no mood to be trifled with. We didn't have a dog to kick, so I was looking for some new family atrocity as an excuse to vent my anger. As I walked in the house, my son asked me if I had gotten a new windowpane for his bedroom. Of course I hadn't—I didn't even know it was broken. Here was the opportunity I was looking for.

"I don't know how you managed to do something so stupid, but you are going to pay for it, young man," I said in an angry, threatening tone.

I was feeling better already.

"I didn't break it. Honest, Dad," he replied hurriedly.

"Where is your brother hiding?"

"He didn't do it either."

"Then who did?" My exasperation was rising to a dangerous level.

"Ask Mom."

I should have known better. There was something in his voice that said, *"Don't* ask Mom," but my frustration overcame my better judgment.

"Judi!" I yelled. "Where are you?"

She said, "Don't yell. I'm right here; what do you want?"

"I want to know—and I want to know *right now*—who broke this window?"

I spoke in my most intimidating tone, a tone that is calculated to cause the children to run to their rooms and cover in mortal terror under their beds—a tone that is also calculated to make their mother cringe and grovel in submission and to speak with the utmost deference for my authority.

"I did," she said. She not only didn't grovel, but there was a definite lack of humility or even apology in her tone. In fact, what she said was, "Do you want to make an issue out of this, buster? Because if you do, I am ready to take some of that 'Blessed Assurance' out of you."

Still angry, but with some restraint, I asked, "How did you do that?"

"*If* it's any of your business," she began in a very defensive tone that said that it most certainly was not any of my business, "it was one of those perfectly normal things that could have happened to anybody—

I was killing a fly."

She stopped there as though that was a perfectly sensible, adequate, and complete explanation. I knew I was treading on dangerous soil, but I plunged ahead. "I don't completely understand exactly how those two things go together," I said timidly.

"Well," she said, with disgust dripping from her voice, "I should have known that it was useless for a *woman* to try to explain anything to a *man*. I suppose I'll have to tell you the whole story."

Very meekly, I apologized for my stupidity and begged her to indulge me.

"Well, after you left I decided to make a pumpkin pie. I had just taken it out of the oven and placed it on the counter to cool. When I went back to check on it, there was a fly walking around on it. That made my blood boil. I tried to shoo it away, but it wouldn't move, so I rolled up a newspaper and hit it. I missed the fly, but I splattered pumpkin pie all over the kitchen. That *really* made me mad. I chased the fly into Lincoln's bedroom, and it landed on the window. I couldn't hit it with the newspaper because it had pumpkin pie on it, and I didn't want to mess up the window, so I took off my shoe and bashed his stupid, miserable brains out with the heel, which broke the stupid, miserable window. Now doesn't that make perfectly good sense?"

As I stood there looking at the broken window, I began to get tickled. The more I thought about my wife—seething with rage, bent upon destruction, hounding her quarry unmercifully, until in desperation the helpless creature, gasping for breath, abandoned any hope of escape and landed on a window to be smashed by a shoe—the funnier it all seemed; and right then I needed a laugh.

I assured my wife that it made perfectly good sense. I applauded her determination and judgment and went to the hardware store to buy a new window.

I laughed for a week.

A good laugh is
sunshine in
a house.

WILLIAM MAKEPEACE THACKERAY

He who provides
for this life,
but takes no care
for eternity,
is wise for a moment,
but a fool forever.

John Tillotson

CROSSING THE GREAT RIVER

After dinner they took the same walk that they always took. The boy knew nearly every step. What he waited for eagerly were the stories his grandfather might tell as things along the way brought back memories. When the boy was small, he had lived quite close to his grandparents, and the Sunday afternoon walks over the farm were regular. Now he lived far away, and he only came during vacations and sometimes on holidays.

"This is where your grandmother and I built our first house; it burned in 1937. If you look carefully, you can still see the corner of the old foundation.

> *That day which you fear as being the end of all things is the birthday of your eternity.*
>
> SENECA

"See the opening there in the barn right under the eave? That's a hay mow. Your father fell out of there, when he was just about your size, and broke his arm." (The stories were much longer, but we have no patience for long stories.)

"Oh, now, Dad," the boy's father interrupted. "He doesn't want to hear that story again; you've told it ten times."

But the boy's father was wrong, and he wasn't only wrong, he wasn't telling the truth. It was he who didn't want to hear the story; it stirred too many painful memories of a happy past—of a life that was so different from his present one—that it didn't seem possible that both lives could have been lived by the same person. The stories reminded him of the contrast between what he had planned and hoped to be and what he had become—

and the contrast was not something

he was comfortable with.

The boy hadn't realized it, and he didn't realize it now, but a sense of the significance of family history and his personal identity had come through those walks and stories. Now he was fourteen, and in his jumbled, confused time of physical and mental transformation, the farm and his grandfather were things that gave meaning and perspective to his growing, changing world. Although he would not have said so, he loved his grandfather,

and he loved the stories.

As they approached the windmill, where the steep ascent to the upper pasture began, his grandfather paused—his thin, white hair matted down with perspiration and his normally clear, blue-gray eyes a little misty. "You and your dad go on up," he said to the boy. "These old legs just won't make it up there anymore. I'll just rest here and wait." That had never happened before, and as the boy and his dad walked slowly away, a thought began to gather in the boy's mind. It gained momentum and clarity as he and his father silently climbed to the pasture. Finally, unable to go farther without hearing his thought aloud, he stopped. He looked at his father and said, "Grandpa's getting old, isn't he, Dad?"

What a world of budding maturity lay behind those words.

"Yes. Dad, your grandpa, is eighty-five this year." The father was not close to his son because he was very busy, and he had not time to tell him stories. Because he didn't know his son, he failed to hear what was behind the question.

"Do you think he minds?"

"Yes, I'm sure he does. He can't do much anymore, and he knows that the good part of his life is behind him." He spoke quickly and with some inner bitterness, as though he did not wish to pursue the topic; but the boy could not turn loose of his thought.

"You'll get old, too, won't you, Dad?"

"Yes, you bet I will. I've already started, and I hate it." Again, the bitterness.

"I can't believe I'll ever get old," the boy said.

"It's hard when you're as young as you are, and all of the good things are in front of you. Why, I remember . . ." he began enthusiastically, but his voice trailed away. The boy turned in anticipation, anxious to hear his father's story, but his father stopped, shrugged his shoulders in resignation, and said, "Oh, forget it."

"Forget what?"

"Nothing; it was nothing. I thought I remembered something there for a minute, but it's gone."

Two hours later they returned to the windmill and found the old man asleep, huddled in a corner out of the wind and where the spring sun would fall on him—a shrunken bundle of faded blue denim and wrinkled flesh. His head lay at a precarious angle, and saliva dripped from the corner of his mouth. His breathing was so shallow that the boy feared he had died, but when he touched his shoulder, the kindly, thoughtful, blue eyes blinked in the sun, and he smiled. As they began the walk back, the boy, still pursuing his thought, expressed his concern.

"Dad says you're eighty-five, Grandpa. Getting old must be terrible. Dad says that the worst thing is that you don't have anything to look forward to, that all the good and important stuff is behind you."

The old man paused and looked long at his son and then at his grandson.

"I think your father has forgotten that I have been preparing for this all my life," he said solemnly. "The most important and the very best things are yet to come, and crossing the great river in front of me is the most important challenge of all."

"River? What river, Grandpa?"

"Ask your father; he knows what river I'm talking about. He needs to remember, and he needs to tell you about it."

Is it time you remembered something that your children need to hear?

But now,
Lord, what do
I look for?
My hope is
in you.

PSALM 39:7

None but God
can satisfy the longing
of the immortal soul;
as the heart
was made for Him,
He only can fill it.

RICHARD CHENEVIX TRENCH

HOME

When I left 736 Clark Road in 1947, it was the only *home* I had ever known. I was ten. I fought the move with every ounce of my being. I left everything I knew, all that was familiar.

My father could never find a resting place after that, and so when I was between the ages of ten and seventeen, we wandered from house to house, town to town, job to job—looking for something my father could not define but thought he would know if he saw. I guess he never saw it—or at least he never recognized it—so he died still looking. I could always tell when it was moving time—the discontent, the restlessness, the bills piling up—the job wasn't working out. It was time to move again. During those years I only knew that *home* was wherever Mom and Dad were, but I had no physical notion of home.

Home was just another temporary stopping place.

After I graduated from high school, I went to Tennessee to go to college. While I was there, Michigan—in some general sense—became home. If anybody asked me where I was from or where my *home* was, I said, "Michigan." My family lived there, and I spent summers there. My sister and brother-in-law moved to Flint, Michigan, in 1956, and they lived there about twenty-five years. Her home became home to me. That's where I spent birthdays and holidays. It's where I went when I was troubled or lonely.

After twenty-five years, they left Michigan and moved to Georgia. Their move left me with a feeling of loneliness and emptiness. Mom and Dad were both dead. There was no reason to ever go back to Michigan. I have nothing there but memories.

Michigan is not *home* anymore.

Some years ago I went back to the place on Clark Road, to show my children where I was raised. The old house was there, but it was much altered. The grape arbor was gone, and the huge pear tree—which had served as a ship, plane, and tank and had carried me on hundreds of adventures—was gone also. The trees had grown, and the chicken coop—into whose wall I smashed my sister's brand-new bicycle—was gone. They had even changed the name of the road from Clark to Creston. Now why would they want to do that? How can a person find *home*, if they change everything?

The swamp below our house, where I turned Pete Vincent's hogs loose, has been drained, and strange people have built houses there—people who neither know nor care that their house is sitting on *my* swamp. They know nothing of me or Pete Vincent's hogs or the marvelous shot my father made, killing a cock pheasant there one winter evening when the swamp was frozen. You see, it was an easy shot at first, but my father's hands were so numb from the cold that he couldn't get the safety off his gun, and the bird was out of range when he finally fired. I watched it sail, with its wings set, all the way to Eighteen Mile Road before it went down. I was sad that he had missed, but he told me he was sure he had hit the bird. I wanted badly to believe him. We walked all the way across the swamp in the gathering darkness, the freezing wind blowing fine flakes of new snow around us. Our dog, Betty, found the bird dead in a clump of marsh grass and cattails.

My father allowed me to carry the gun on the way home, and I walked close to him, knowing that surely no boy had as fine a father as I.

But the swamp is gone,

and so is my father.

During the intervening years, I have followed my father's pattern—moving from house to house, town to town, job to job. I always knew that I was looking for something. I didn't know exactly what it was, but I knew I would know it if I saw it. I have never seen it, and now I know *why. It is not here!* I am not going to *find it*—it will *find me.*

When I cross the Great River and open my eyes on the other side, I will know that this is it—that I am finally and forever home—that every tree, every building, every rock, and blade of grass is exactly where it ought to me, where I always knew it would be. And I will say,

"Why, here it is—

yes, this is it exactly."

Life is
a voyage that's
homeward bound.

HERMAN MELVILLE

Because your
love is
better than life,
my lips
will glorify you.

Psalm 63:3

A good name
is more desirable than
great riches;
to be esteemed
is better than silver
or gold.

PROVERBS 22:1

Stories of times gone by instill in us a consciousness
of who we are—they give us a sense of *history*,
and they help us connect the past with the future.

Write your own story here, then share it with someone you love.

Printed in the United States
By Bookmasters